Not Without a Struggle

Not Without a
Struggle

LEADERSHIP DEVELOPMENT
FOR AFRICAN AMERICAN
WOMEN IN MINISTRY

VASHTI M. MCKENZIE

United Church Press
Cleveland, Ohio

United Church Press, Cleveland, Ohio 44115
© 1996 by Vashti M. McKenzie

01 00 99 98 97 96 5 4 3 2

Library of Congress Cataloging-in-Publication Data

McKenzie, Vashti M., 1947
    Not without a struggle : leadership development for African
American women in ministry / Vashti M. McKenzie.
        p. cm.
    Includes bibliographical references.
    ISBN 0-8298-1076-5 (alk. paper)
    1. Afro-American women clergy—Training of. 2. Christian
leadership. I. Title.
BR563.N4M35   1996
262'.14'082—dc20   96-26237
                                                            CIP

To my husband, Stan,
and our children,
Jon-Mikael, Vashti-Jasmine, and Joi-Marie

And to my first female leader, my mother,
Ida Murphy Peters
"Be strong, we are not here to drift or dream . . ."

CONTENTS

PREFACE

Not Without a Struggle is more than a book by one woman about some women. It is a compilation of thoughts inspired by the lives and experiences of extraordinary women who dared to believe God. They believed God instead of the limiting social and cultural dictates of their generation. They believed God instead of the interpretation tradition of man. They believed God's intention for their lives and ministry even when others tried to use this same God to keep them silent and secluded.

Not Without a Struggle is more than the effort of one woman. It is the product of the many men and women who shared their expertise, wisdom, stories, and experiences. They mentored, tutored, and pushed me, especially when pushing was needed! They gave me opportunities too numerous to mention.

Not Without a Struggle began long before the time nearly twenty years ago when God began to stir my heart. It began long before I ever knew my grandmother—institution initiator—orator, Vashti Turley Murphy, or my mother—marketing/advertising pioneer, Ida Murphy Peters, who at age seventy-seven still writes a weekly column for a major newspaper (and wouldn't dream of missing a day at the office, all of course not without a struggle).

Is it possible that these thoughts began in a garden, were derailed by a serpent, prophesied by Joel (Joel 2:28), nailed on a cross, resurrected from a grave, included by a Savior (Galatians 3:28), and preached by Peter (Acts 2:17–21) to be lived by God's called-out women?

Not Without a Struggle is our humble offering to the growing body of literature about and for women in ministry in general, and African American women in ministry in particular.

Acknowledgments

IT WAS A tremendous honor to be an H. Beecher Hicks Scholar in United Theological Seminary's doctor of ministry program in Dayton, Ohio. A major portion of this work was developed under Dr. Hicks's valuable leadership and guidance. United's Dr. Darryl Ward and Dr. Mary Olsen gave tremendous support and insight.

Cain Hope Felder is a taskmaster and one of the finest biblical scholars in this country. Dr. Felder was a fountain of wisdom, advice, and encouragement. Thanks to him for opening doors for all of his students! Dr. Jeremiah Wright continually provides information and inspiration. Many thanks to Drs. Jacquelyn Grant, Suzan Johnson Cook, Barbara Lucas, Jessica Ingram, and Renita Weems Espinoza for being kingdom women role models for me and countless others.

I must thank my father and mother in the ministry, Bishop John Bryant and Rev. Cecilia Williams Bryant; Bishop John Hurst Adams, for his call for excellence and education; Bishop H. Hartford Brookins, for having the confidence that God can use a female preacher to serve Payne Memorial AME Church; Bishop D. Ward Nichols, for his wealth of wisdom; Bishop Frederick Calhoun James, the presidng prelate of the Second Episcopal District, for his steadfast faith and support; and our episcopal forebears in God, who share their hopes and dreams for our Zion now and in the twenty-first century.

I thank my sisters in public service, who blessed me to serve as the spiritual leader of 195,000 college-trained women in a service organization "founded upon Christian principles."

Ms. N. Cajetta Stephens and Mrs. Delores Williams spent many hours typing and retyping this work. Rev. Angelique Mason and the Daughters of Zion of Payne Memorial undergirded this effort with prayer and encouragement. Special thanks to the staff and volunteers of Payne Memorial, who carried extra weight, and to a loving congregation, who patiently heard the genesis of this research and shared experiences.

I also wish to acknowledge the women in ministry who attended the original Women Surviving in Ministry seminar in 1992. Many other women across the nation heard about this project and supported it with their long-distance participation via mail, telephone, and faxes.

My husband, Stan McKenzie, has lived with this body of thoughts longer than anyone. He has been supportive and sacrificing through two degree programs, three pregnancies (two while in seminary), and many long nights reading or writing. Our children, Jon-Mikael, Vashti-Jasmine, and Joi-Marie, shared this experience with us, and we are eternally grateful for three talented servants of God.

Kim Sadler, Ed Huddleston, and the production staff of United Church Press are the most patient publishers in the world!

I thank God for the named and unnamed shoulders I stand upon—the women in the pulpit and the pew who dared to believe God's will for their lives. They laid a tremendous foundation for this generation. Pray that we will be able to leave a legacy as rich and daring.

INTRODUCTION

"And your daughters shall prophesy . . ."

—Acts 2:17

IT WAS MY SECOND Sunday as pastor of Payne Memorial A.M.E. Church, a congregation rich in history and long on tradition. It was the first time in the church's ninety-three-year history that a woman had served as pastor.

An elderly member of the church approached me as I left the pulpit. She reached beyond my extended hand to hug and kiss me on the cheek. "I was one of the ones who didn't want a woman pastor. I've changed my mind. I'm glad you're my pastor!" she said. Her husband smiled and nodded "yes" behind her.

Five months later, I had just made my first pastoral report from Payne Memorial at the Baltimore Annual Conference when Bishop H. Hartford Brookins, then presiding prelate of the Second Episcopal District of the A.M.E. Church, asked another senior member and officer of the church how he liked his new pastor. "We love her just fine," waving his hand in the bishop's direction.

These two experiences were initial indications that a paradigm shift was in progress. "Paradigm" simply means "pattern," from the Greek word *paradeigma*. The pattern contains the attitudes, thoughts, and behaviors that make up a person's lifestyle. Like the pattern used to cut pieces of cloth for a garment, the pattern defines the boundaries of the pieces and indicates how to assemble them successfully; it constitutes the rules and regulations for sewing the garment. In order to change the garment or to accommodate changes in the wearer, such as size, weight, and height, a new pattern must be made.

The paradigm or pattern in the cultural societal sense, therefore, is the blueprint for how a person assembles the pieces of their lives. Changes in a person's life exert pressure on the pattern. The pattern can either shift to adapt to a new reality or remain stationary, inhibiting change.[1]

For many centuries the pattern from which the garment of pastoral leadership was constructed did not include any pieces that allowed clergywomen to be sewn into the prophetic leadership fabric of congregational life. What was taking place at Payne Memorial and countless other congregations across the country was the redesign of the pattern for pastoral service. The pattern is not a new one: Its structure was drawn from the holy writ (Joel 2:28, Acts 2:17, and Gal. 3:27–28), was distorted by sexism, and reemerges as a new idea.

Reclaiming the past to design a new future brings with it a certain amount of stress and emotional response. The reclamation fosters role changes that threaten values deeply embedded in the personality. Any change becomes a threat to the person and is often viewed as a destructive force that subverts the paradigm of social values.[2]

I smile, remembering those two early encounters of paradigm shift at Payne Memorial. I also remember the anxious moments of pattern shifting in the one rural church and the other urban church in which I served. Each of these congregations had never previously experienced female pastoral leadership. All three emerged with a new sense of egalitarianism, a mutual partnership that respects the unique differences in gender. *Different* becomes *unique,* not inferior or superior.[3]

The Bible is filled with paradigm busters, men and women who redesigned the patterns of religion, society, and culture. There were many who desired to obey God rather than human beings (Acts 5:29):

- *Moses was a paradigm buster:* He challenged the existing hierarchical arrangement between slave and master and between the Israelites and the Egyptians. He used leadership skills to bring pressure to bear on an intolerable condition (Exod. 3–14).
- *Deborah was a paradigm buster:* In God's list of judges, there was a left-handed man; an illegitimate son; an erratic, unstable strong man; one "least of his father's house"; and a prophet named Deborah. She used leadership skills to be God's woman, exercising authority in civil and military affairs (Judg. 4–5).

- *Nehemiah was a paradigm buster:* He used leadership skills to effectively rebuild the Jerusalem wall after the Babylonian captivity. He remained connected to God through prayer, dealing effectively with opposition and promotion (Neh. 4–8).
- *Esther was a paradigm buster:* She emerged as the Lord's agent of change inside the palace of King Ahasuerus. Within her role as queen consort, her leadership skills were developed quietly out of public view but under the tutelage of God. At the critical time, she broke through "for such as time as this" to deliver her people from extermination.
- *The woman at the well was a paradigm buster:* The intentional encounter between Jesus and this Samaritan woman broke down racial and gender barriers. She dropped her water pots and became the evangelist to Sychar (John 4).

History reflects many female paradigm busters. The roll of women breaking into all-male paradigms such as business, politics, sports, and religion is not a new story. Some of the women who have effectively stormed the heights of exclusionary social paradigms include Madame C. J. Walker, entrepreneur; Shirley Chisholm, presidential candidate; Mary McCloud Bethune, presidential adviser; Carol Mosely Braun, U.S. senator; Rev. Pauli Murray, first Episcopal priest; Bishop Leontyne Kelly, retired United Methodist episcopate; Lena Horne, entertainer; Oprah Winfrey, entertainment entrepreneur. But they did not achieve their accomplishments without a struggle!

The new story is the fact that women are bringing pressure to bear on all-male paradigms in such great numbers.[4] Significantly, women are not merely redesigning the pattern but are surviving and succeeding. The impact of millions of women competing in the same job market for the same jobs—including pulpits, appointments, denominational positions, and tenure in seminaries—exerts a tremendous impact on the tapestry of religious life. Millions of women all over the world are challenging existing power patterns, infusing them with more humanistic values.[5]

The influx of women into leadership positions in the church and church-related professions is on the rise. Women are serving as bishops, presiding elders, district superintendents, pastors, elders, deacons, chaplains, pastoral counselors, campus ministers, seminary professors, and denominational officers.

Women are pushing for inclusive language, presenting feminist and womanist views in scholarly work, developing all-woman churches, services, and ministries. Statistical data on women in ministry are few.[6] While statistics on women pastors in mainline Eurocentric denominations are limited, they are even sketchier in predominantly African American denominations. Yet we know that by 1993 the United Church of Christ had ordained approximately 1,800 women; the United Methodist Church had ordained 4,200; the Presbyterian Church, 2,419; 1,000 of the 14,000 clergy in the Episcopal Church were women; the Evangelical Lutheran Church in America had 1,429 clergywomen; 1,000 of the 14,000 ministers in the Disciples of Christ were women; and, in 1988, about one-third of the 19,000 ordained clergy in the African Methodist Episcopal Church were women. According to figures from the National Council of Churches (which have not been updated since 1986), there are 20,730 women clergy. That figure represents a 21,000 increase over 1977 data. At that time, there were 5,591 licensed women. There are approximately 30,000 clergywomen in the United States. By the late 1990s, that figure may increase by as much as another 12,000.[7]

An indication of the dramatic increase of women in the ministry is reflected in the deluge of women entering seminary. According to Joseph O'Neill of the Educational Testing Service in Princeton, New Jersey, an unprecedented one-third of the 56,000 students in seminary are women.[8]

In the 1992–93 school year at Howard University School of Divinity, approximately 42 percent of the students were women. At Harvard Divinity School, 60 percent of the student population were women. At Yale, approximately 30 percent of enrolled students were women.[9]

The African American church is just beginning to challenge sexism as a serious social concern. Women of African descent in North America are pioneering equal access to ordained ministry, professional training, preparation, and promotion. There are perhaps more African American women serving as pastors and preachers than White women.[10] In 1973, African American women made up 5 percent of students enrolled in seminary. By 1984, women represented 20 percent of the total African American enrollment.[11] Although only about 5 percent of clergy in the seven mainline African American denominations are women, there were about 5,000 ordained women in independent and storefront churches. Some of the women led more than one congregation, and others served as bishops.[12]

More does not necessarily mean *better.* Just because there are more women answering the call to the gospel ministry does not make challenging the paradigm of male-dominated ministry any easier. On the contrary, the problems of African American women are often like a double-barreled shotgun: racism and sexism.

A study of African American female religious professionals reveals that an overwhelming majority report that they are still treated with suspicion and indifference. They experience a lack of support and are heavily exploited. Yet they remain confident of their qualifications to minister, even if God is their only supporter.[13]

African American clergywomen have found the strength to challenge existing social paradigms based upon the dominance of one gender over another. They are challenging patterns that fly in the face of a liberating Christ, who busted the distinctions of race, gender, and ethnic origin as a means of inclusion.

Not Without a Struggle traces the thread of female leadership in Roman, Greek, Jewish, and African cultures. The book briefly focuses upon the historical threads of female leadership in the church. The intent is to help women in general, and African American women in particular, to understand that they are not accidents, freaks, flukes, or mistakes in the dominion of God. A minister who happens to be a woman is not an individual who just stumbled into leadership because no one else was available; she is part of a historical legacy.

This book reviews some of the theological patterns that reject and support female leadership. It also looks at the images of female leadership in the Bible as well as in other ancient sources.

Sixty-four African American women in ministry were surveyed in the Women Surviving in Ministry seminar and project, and one hundred additional women were interviewed about twenty-eight questions on a variety of topics including education, leadership, church, and personal and spiritual life. Admittedly, the survey and interviews are limited by region and denomination. It is, however, a valuable assemblage of ideas, experiences, behaviors, and habits of contemporary African American clergywomen. Their responses can be used for further dialogue among clergywomen and between men and women laboring together in God's ministerial vineyard.

Leadership by minorities (Hispanics, African Americans, women) is not only necessary but demanded in all ministerial roles—pastors, teachers, counselors. Leadership is the powerful force by which exclusionary paradigms such as racism and sexism may be confronted, challenged, and changed.

Leaders work on existing paradigms; managers work within existing paradigms. Leaders identify the right things to do; managers do the right things right. Leaders, for the most part, pursue goals and press forward while managers are the stewards of the human and physical resources necessary to achieve the goal and to maintain it after it has been achieved. Rosa Parks was a leader who sat down in the front of the bus and effectively challenged the Jim Crow–era paradigm. Martin Luther King Jr. effectively busted the "separate but equal" paradigm by exerting leadership in the civil rights movement. Marian Wright Edelman challenges existing social paradigms that endanger children. The selection of Barbara Harris as Bishop Suffragant in the Episcopal Church broke through the existing paradigm of excluding women from upper-denominational leadership. The mere presence of a woman in the pulpit represents a challenge to existing exclusionary paradigms in the church.

Not Without a Struggle shares lessons in leadership gathered from interviews and surveys with African American clergywomen from across the country. It explores biblical role models, leadership styles, and offers an example of womanist-leader behaviors for African American women.

Although this book does not deal with all of the issues facing African American clergy, it does provide "Ten Commandments for Women in the Ministry" to serve as a leadership resource. *Not Without a Struggle* prayerfully provides some answers and leaves more than an oral record for the "daughters of thunder" who will come behind me.

Not Without a Struggle

HISTORICAL PERSPECTIVES ON FEMALE LEADERSHIP IN GREEK, ROMAN, AND JEWISH CULTURE AND RELIGION

THE TAPESTRY OF female leadership is woven with threads centuries old. A glimpse of the historical threads of female leadership in Greek, Roman, and Jewish societies reminds us that women exercised leadership behaviors and responsibilities in spite of structures of oppression, silence, and seclusion. Women did not have the privilege of leadership training and preparation. Rabbis taught their daughters the Torah in secret. Huldah prophesied and Deborah judged when women in their era were denied formal education.

Many societies relegated women to the fringes of community life. Their roles were defined, for the most part, along a patriarchal system and were limited to childbearing and housekeeping responsibilities. Women were treated in some traditions as property, to be counted along with the acres of land, houses, and cattle. This is certainly true of ancient Jewish society.

The problem of examining these historical threads is the use and recovery of sources. Many of them were recorded by males displaying biases typical of their society. Sources authored by women also preserved a male cultural paradigm.[1]

Womanist and feminist biblical scholars, theologians, and history scholars, such as Jacqueline Grant, Virginia Mollenkott, Rosemary Ruether, Renita Weems, Katie Cannon, and Eleanor McLaughlin, have endeavored to retrieve women's views and roles without looking through the lens of patriarchal systems. The desire is to elevate the experiences of these foremothers long buried because of neglect and female marginalization.

The contribution of women to the growth and development of

their society and religious life emerges from a variety of sources. These sources include diaries, letters, literature, art, historical accounts, journals, the Bible, and other writings considered sacred by various religious groups.

There are those, such as H. Wayne House in *The Role of Women in Ministry Today*, who believe that to do this undermines the traditional role of women in society and the church. Paradigm changes in major institutions such as the church move slowly because the values of the institution are deeply embedded into their personalities and those of their participants. Any change that threatens the values of the paradigm threatens the personality, often causing an intense emotional response.[2]

When one has a vested interest in a person, group, or institution remaining the same, one views change as a negative rather than a positive. Change is also viewed as destroying the fabric of social values that undergird an institution, society, person, or group.[3] This is reflected not only in the recording and interpreting of history but in the hermeneutics of biblical interpretation.

History often interprets women as the weaker sex or even the lesser sex. The Bible and history of interpretation give a similar portrait. But neither the Bible nor history denies that women—by personality, gifts, skills, or charisma—have contributed much to their societies and the growth of the church.[4]

Therefore, unless we reconstruct the experiences of foremothers from available sources, we leave a wealth of contributions and history undisclosed. We also deny the role that individual women played in the evolving ecclesia.

The challenge is to bring forward and identify positive images of female leadership and at the same time destroy the myth of "otherness": the assumption that women are peripheral and secondary historical objects of church and community life—the others (Luke 8:3, 24:1, Acts 17:34). Making the historical threads of female leadership visible presents an opportunity for others to analyze the compilation.[5]

Another challenge is to avoid being caught in subjective biases in recovering roles and relationships from the past. Women were empowered to provide leadership even as they struggled in circumstances deemed demeaning by today's cultural attitudes.

The historical framework of female leadership must have a dual tension. It requires a balancing act between making women visible and discerning insights into oppressive systems.[6]

Female leadership roles can be discerned even in material that was controlled by ideologies that redacted women's roles and views to make them reflect prescribed societal norms. Women who fit a society's determined sex-role patterns were lifted up as indisputable role models. However, if a woman's role or actions did not measure up to the society's norms, her view or role might be deleted from the sources, or she might be portrayed as an archetype of dissent. A few examples follow:

- Hypatis, an Afro-Egyptian, did not fit the ancient Greek paradigm for female behavior. She wrote and lectured at the University of Alexandria on philosophy, mathematics, physics, and astronomy.[7]
- Thecla did not fit the paradigm for women in Palestine, and her name and missionary journeys with Paul barely survived the editing of some first-century writers.
- Phoebe did not fit the pattern either, and little more than her name and title of *diakonos*, or "deacon," survive in Romans 16:1.
- Women were excluded from the rabbinic, yet writings of a rabbi named Beruria survives.
- Women teachers in the Protestant tradition did not fit the pattern and were branded as heretics in the nineteenth century. For example, when a group of ordained women under the leadership of Elizabeth Cady Stanton gathered in 1890 to write a biblical commentary, male ministers called their actions a collaboration between "women and the devil."

In spite of source and methodology problems, women appear to have had a multiplicity of authoritative leadership roles in Greece, Rome, and Jewish societies. Female leadership is not a new issue, and neither are the struggles and challenges female leaders face.

THE STATUS OF WOMEN IN ANCIENT GREEK SOCIETY

"The woman was a Greek, a Syrophoenician by nation . . . " (Mark 7:26)

Women in ancient Greece and Rome lived between two extremes. One was the ideal patriarchal role of the obedient silent wife working in the home in seclusion. The other was the woman who challenged the ideal of male dominance and superiority. Often she was wealthy, owned property, and exercised a role in political and religious society. This tension of opposites adds a "yes, but . . ." character to the complex social world of the Mediterranean preceding and during the time of Jesus.

800 B.C.E.

There has been much discussion among scholars about whether the earliest social structures of Greece were matriarchal[8] (meaning either that men and women were equal or that men were subordinate to women). In any case, it seems that in the religious hierarchy, the ancient Greek goddesses dominated.

Zeus, described as a heroic male god, gained power and established a patriarchal order among the gods. Hesiod's "Theogony" written around 700 B.C.E. describes the power paradigm shift.[9]

Homeric epics written in the eighth century B.C.E. include powerful and influential queens such as Helen, Clytemnestra, and Penelope. Power and authority were passed not from father to son but rather matrilineally, from mother to daughter.

Homer tended to portray women within his own patriarchal values. Women were secluded and confined to the home and domestic responsibilities. Upper-class women had slaves to do menial tasks. While wives were praised for their fidelity, men were allowed to be polygamous and have slave concubines.[10]

Mycenian tablets reveal differences between food allotments for men and women. Men received twice as much food as women, perhaps indicating that women occupied positions inferior to men.[11]

Hesiod viewed women as the embodiment of evil. This is reflected in the story of Pandora, who according to Greek mythology brought sin upon mankind. Thus, Pandora is cast in the same negative role as the biblical Eve.[12]

800–500 B.C.E.

The legal codes of Sparta reveal that the most important role of women in the archaic city-state around the seventh century B.C.E. was to bear children. This was the reason they were given equal food rations. Spartan women were also educated and trained in athletics. Women of the upper class left menial tasks to lower-class women, thus freeing their time for gymnastics, music, household management, and childrearing.

Women obtained the right to control, inherit, and own property, according to the law codes of Gortyna on Crete. In a divorce, a woman could keep half her property.

Several women distinguished themselves as poets during this period. Some, like Sappho and Corinna, are well known; others' names have been forgotten, but their work survives.

500–323 B.C.E.

The "yes, but . . ." dichotomy between the patriarchal ideal and the women who challenged it is evident in the classical period in Athens. There is evidence that there was definite sex-role differentiation. Women were, for the most part, prohibited from participating in politics and education. But, they were not totally secluded, as they attended festivals, funerals, and perhaps even the theater. In Plutarch's writings about the customs and mores of this period, there are references to poets and prophets.[13]

The primary responsibilities of women during this period were to bear children and to strengthen the family unit. Parents arranged marriages for their daughters when the girls were in their early teens, giving the son-in-law a dowry as a means of supporting his wife. These funds remained intact during the marriage, with the husband receiving an annual interest percentage.

A daughter could inherit if no son was born to the union. She would then be obligated to immediately marry her next male kin. In case of divorce, which could be initiated by either party, the children were the property of the husband.

Women of this era had little time for education. They had their hands full with slaves, children, a home, and often a separate women's quarters. When the husband entertained guests, the wife was not allowed to be present.

Attitudes about women's roles in society are deeply rooted in written and oral history passed from ancient Greek and Roman literature. Euripides portrayed several women, such as Polyxena and Alcestis, as self-sacrificing heroines. Aristotle, on the other hand, wrote that the law of nature decreed women to be inferior to men.[14] Pericles is quoted as saying that the best reputation a woman could have is that men do not speak of her for good or evil.[15]

"Yes, but . . ." women were nonetheless literate, had some understanding of politics and economics, and were allowed to testify in court.

HELLENISM

The conquests of Alexander the Great bought the Greek city-states to a conclusion. As society changed, so did the role and status of women in the new emerging empire.

Women were granted the opportunity to conduct business, make loans, and manumit slaves with permission of their guardians. In Egypt, another region of the empire, women could make wills, sign contracts, and pay taxes.

The Hellenistic queens operated with real political power in Syria, Egypt, and Greece. Women exercised their leadership skills in their own right. They also held leadership positions because of absent or weak husbands. When a king died leaving a male heir too young to rule, the mother queen held the throne for him. Queen Plympias ruled Greece while her son, Alexander the Great, was away. Arsinoe II ruled Egypt with her husband, and Cleopatra VII ruled toward the end of the period.

Women did not gain political rights and a voice in social affairs through philosophy or social reform, but rather through economics. Women used their personal wealth to build improvements such as reservoirs, roads, and aqueducts. Women in Sparta owned 40 percent of all land. Other women exercised their skills in poetry, literature, education, music, medicine, crafts, and philosophy. Women used real political and economic power as the pathways to leadership, freedom, and equality. They used their possessions to challenge social ideals and the patriarchal system. Some women gained equal status with men.[16]

"Yes, but . . ." marriages were still arranged, even for queens, to secure political alliances. Sisters were married to brothers to strengthen the family unit. In the case of divorce, the husband kept the community property. Men could take concubines, and prostitution was legal.

The Stoic and Neopythagorean schools of philosophy emphasized traditional sex roles and the exclusion of women. The Cynics and Epicureans included women on an equal level in their schools. Hipparchia was a Cynic philosopher who lectured publicly with her husband.

FEMALE LEADERSHIP IN ANCIENT AND HELLENISTIC GREEK RELIGION

Ancient Greek and Hellenistic art depicts women either as goddesses or priestesses—objects to be worshiped or leaders of ceremonies and rituals. They were ornately dressed and danced as a part of religious cults.

When Zeus became the chief god, the role of women goddesses became subordinate to men in Greek religion. Male priests became part of the rites of goddesses to the point of dominating them. Some cults also arose that denied participation by women altogether.

Pythia, a middle-aged celibate, chosen and trained by male priests, served as a woman priest at Delphi. She spoke in a trance often enhanced by drugs, and male priests interpreted her gibberish.[17] The role of the female priest of Athena Polias was hereditary, filled by a member of a prominent noble family.

The rise of the mystery cults began in the Hellenistic period. Several cults allowed women full participation, and some cults were exclusively or primarily practiced by women. There were state and private cults that attracted men and women. The opportunity to participate in cults, and in their leadership, probably contributed to the conversion of many women to these syncretic religions.

A factor contributing to the influx of women into these cults was that some women found the traditional social roles of this period too confining.[18] This point is significant to keep in mind when we meet similar criticism of widespread female participation and leadership in Montanism, asceticism, and sects outside of mainstream Protestantism.

As new cults became more accepted and visible, their membership began to be drawn more from the upper-class, established groups. The cults would then be pressured to emphasize more-traditional values and roles. Thus, female participation and leadership once again would be suppressed.[19]

THE STATUS OF WOMEN IN THE ROMAN EMPIRE

"And so we went toward Rome." (Acts 28:14)

In the Roman empire, traditional sex roles were practiced. "Yes, but . . ." tension was ever present between the patriarchal ideal and the historical woman, who moved independently in the marketplace and in political circles.

Women were under the complete control of "paterfamilias," according to Roman law. These male heads of an extended family exercised life-and-death power over their charges. They arranged marriages and conducted all family business. The death penalty could be given to a woman for drinking alcohol or adultery.[20]

During the time of Augustus, a free woman was no longer under the control of the paterfamilias after the birth of her third child. She could also appeal her guardian's decisions to a magistrate or request a new guardian. At times during the Augustan period, women could conduct their own business affairs because the law of the guardians was not strictly enforced.

Women usually were married between the ages of twelve and fifteen. Divorce could be initiated by either party or even by the wife's father. Children became the property of the husband. Daughters were not given individual names but rather the feminine form of their father's name. If none existed, they were given a number. Women had the right to inherit and often amassed great fortunes. Infanticide was also practiced during this time.

"Yes, but . . . ," in spite of this oppression, there are indications that women used their finances to win recognition and prestige within their communities. They participated actively in manufacturing and commerce, as did men.[21]

Ancient writer Pomeroy notes that the women of the eastern provinces who were freed women traded in luxury items such as perfumes and purple dyes. That fact should be remembered when we meet Lydia, a seller of purple goods in Acts. There was also Eumachia, who used money from a brick manufacturing enterprise to finance a major building. Mamia is credited with building the temple of the Genius of Augustus.[22]

These women were hardly silent or secluded. They were able to break through the traditional roles of their time not because others perceived their business acumen, commerce aptitude, skill, or intellect, but purely by economic means. They had the finances to purchase equality. No sense of equality or fairness opened closed doors to the women—only money, which is recognized as an equalizer for many minorities in various cultures and at various times.

FEMALE LEADERSHIP IN ROMAN RELIGION

Women had an official role in religion in the Roman empire, but they were excluded from the highest religious offices. Whether the cults admitted only women or both men and women, they were ultimately controlled by men. Often, even in women-only cults, male leaders used the cult religion to reinforce patriarchal ideals.

The objectification of women is seen in Rome's choice of Vesta—the goddess of the continuity of the family, state, and domesticity—as the official head of its state cult. Nevertheless, the highest leadership offices were not open to women. The leadership included the all-male *"pontifex maximus"* and a college of pontiffs.

Women participated as ornaments in rituals. Ornaments or objects are auxiliary to the ritual but do not occupy the seat of power within the ritual. Although an automobile's hood ornament is important for identification and beauty, the real power is not in the hood ornament but in the engine beneath it. Similarly, the white linen that tradition-ally adorns altars in some Christian traditions during Holy Communion, is an important aspect of the ritual. However, the real power is beneath the linen—in the consecrated bread and wine. You can drive a car without a hood ornament; you can partake in Holy Communion without the white linen. But neither the car nor the Eucharist will go very far without the engine or the elements.

In much the same way, women participate as ornaments in modern religious rituals. Today, women in many religions are allowed to carry, prepare, protect, read, and decorate sacred objects and instruments of ritual. For example, women are allowed to participate fully, even in leadership roles, as worship acolytes, lay readers, or members of altar guilds that maintain the altar and altar paraments. A recent "conces-sion" of the pope in the Catholic tradition is to allow girls to be serv-ers at Mass.

In the Methodist tradition, at one time women were not allowed to serve as spiritual leaders of the church or stewards. Stewards, appointed by the pastor, had responsibilities pertaining to the provisions for the pastor and the finances of the church. However, rather than appoint women as stewards, an auxiliary role of stewardess was developed. The stewardesses were allowed to prepare, carry, and decorate the altar for the disposition of the sacraments of Holy Communion. They were appointed to the position but did not have any responsibility for pastoral provision or church finances. Stewardesses today perform a valuable function which must not be diminished in any way. But we must recognize that their role was developed as an auxiliary to leadership.

In other Christian traditions, women are allowed to carry, even read from the Bible, but not preach from it; clean and decorate the pulpit but not sit in it; raise money for the church but not participate in the decision of how it is spent; or be pretty in the pew rather than intelligent in the boardroom.

Roman women participated as vestal virgins, guardians of the sacred flame. Virgins were beaten publicly for letting the fire go out and buried alive for sexual misconduct. Until the time of Augustus, vestal virgins were selected from patrician families, beginning at the age of six or ten and usually serving for thirty years. At retirement they could marry, but often did not because of their age. Many continued in office, enjoying great power and authority. These women were the only female citizens who were independent of the paterfamilias.

There were some cults that admitted only men, such as Hercules, and some that admitted only women, such as Bona Dea. There were cults defined by social or marital class. The cult of Womanly Fortune included patrician women. The cult of Patrician Chastity was for patrician women only; and the cult of Virile Fortune was for prostitutes only.

THE STATUS OF WOMEN IN JEWISH SOCIETY

Woman is introduced as the "helpmeet" of man in Genesis 2:20. From this Yahwist account of creation and later in Genesis 3, the fall, it is often interpreted that from the very beginning a woman was created second, insubordinate to man and the cause of evil in the world.[23]

In the Priestly creation account in Genesis 1, woman is introduced as being created at the same time as man. Both imaged God, and both received commission and blessing.[24]

The Hebrew laws provide us with information about the status of women. Women's dominant role was in the arena of domestic responsibilities, involving home and motherhood. A mother was to be obeyed (Deut. 21:18), feared (Lev. 19:3), and honored (Exod. 20:12). She not only named the children but was responsible for their early education. She brought sacrificial offerings to assemblage for worship.[25]

A Hebrew woman's identity was derived from her marital status and reproductive fruitfulness. Women were considered the property of men—either their fathers or their husbands. A widow was the property of her next of kin. In Exodus 20:17, a woman was listed among the property that one should not covet. The mother of a son was held in high esteem. Barren women were thought to be cursed or out of favor with God. The Talmud would later sum up the purpose of women in marriage in solely domestic terms, bearing children and being beautiful wives.[26]

The Authorized Daily Prayer Book, used by worshipers in the synagogue, reveals one of the prevailing attitudes about women. The men, in their prayers, blessed God for not creating them female; the women blessed God for creating them according to divine will.[27]

The patriarchal family system also kept women silent and secluded. Their heads were covered and faces veiled when they were in the presence of others. The women were not allowed to eat with guests. Conversation between men and women was discouraged.[28]

"Yes, but . . . ," some women were active outside of the home (Prov. 31, and Anna in Tobit 2:11–12). There were also heroines such as Esther, Judith, and the mother in 2 Maccabees 7, who died under the persecution of Antiochus with her seven sons.

Philo, a Jewish philosopher, believed that women were evil and inferior to men. Historian Josephus also espoused the theoretical inferiority of women. Yet he mentioned a number of influential women in his writings.[29]

Although women themselves were not permitted to receive formal education, they were responsible for the instruction of children up to a certain age. Women may have been allowed some education in religious issues; it seems that Lois, Eunice, and Priscilla received some religious orientation (2 Tim. 1:5; Acts 18:18–26).

"Yes, but . . ." although women were considered inferior and subservient, a few emerged as leaders, making contributions to commu-

nity and God's plan of salvation. Functioning in their role in the patriarchal system, several women emerge as valuable contributors to community life. Women are mentioned in Old Testament literature as sages
and wise women whose counsel was sought (2 Sam. 14:2–20; 20:15–
22; Judg. 5:29). Women also wrote hymns, notably the Song of Miriam
(Exod. 15:21) and the Song of Deborah (Judg. 5). These women tran-
scended the silent and secluded ideal: Miriam was a prophet, and
Deborah served as a judge of all Israel.

FEMALE LEADERSHIP IN RELIGIOUS LIFE

In Judaic life during the Old and New Testament times, women participated only marginally in religious life. They were not required to
make pilgrimages to Jerusalem for major festivals. They could not study
the Torah or recite prayers at meals. Women were not counted in the
minyan, the quorum of persons needed for worship to take place. In
theory, any adult person could read or preach in the synagogue. In
practice, however, women were kept physically separated from men in
worship.[30]

In the rabbinic tradition, boys were taught to be rabbis, teachers,
and transmitters of tradition. Women were excluded; however, there
were a few rabbis who ignored the tradition and taught Torah to their
daughters.[31]

No surviving resources indicate any woman having served in a
priestly office. One often-cited reason is that women were considered
ritually unclean during menses and childbirth, excluding them from
participating in temple ritual at these times. Their touch was thought
to contaminate others.[32]

In spite of societal limitations and the dim view of women's skills
and talents, the Old Testament bears witness to the important role
individual women played in religious life. Such women as Miriam,
Deborah, Huldah, the wife of Isaiah, Noadiah, and Anna served as
prophets. Deborah was not only a prophet but a judge who served as a
ruling head of all Israel during the confederation period for forty years.
An exception to the seclusion rule, this married woman also led as a
military commander in battle (Judg. 4–5).

Other women also served as leaders; they were used by God instru-
mentally if not necessarily in religious life. Esther and Jezebel were

both queens wielding great influence. Queen Athaliah ruled the Southern Kingdom when her son Ahaziah died.

There were several women who served as unofficial leaders, without title or official positions, but who demonstrated spiritual influence and/or goodwill. One example is the woman at the well in John 4. Jesus broke through barriers of race and gender to engage here in an intentional conversation in Samaria. Without a recorded name or ordination, the woman evangelized Sychar. There was Mary Magdalene, Mary the mother of James, and Salome, who first received the resurrection victory message and were told to tell (Matt. 28:7; Mark 16:7; Luke 24:10; John 20:18).

The Judaic community appears to have been willing to allow individual women to be exceptions to their patriarchal ideal but to have been unwilling to give the gender credit for gifts, skills, talent, and the call of God. *One* extraordinary woman did not change a cultural mindset in that era. Today, *some* extraordinary women still find it difficult to change cultural biases against women in nontraditional roles.

Chapter two

Historical Perspectives on Female Leadership in African Culture and Religion

"Behold, a man of Ethiopia, a eunuch of great authority under Candace queen of the Ethiopians . . ." (Acts 8:27)

African American clergywomen and African American women in general have a rich legacy of African female leadership role models. Unlike their counterparts in Greek, Roman, and Jewish societies, African women served as partners with men, shaping kingdoms and community life. Women were more included in the leadership of ancient African cultures.

Women were goddesses, scribes, Great Wives, queen regents for too-young heirs, queen mothers, queen warriors, and queens exercising authoritative leadership in their own right. Women served as military leaders, academic professors, and community leaders.

The theory and practice of female inferiority and subservience were far more prevalent in Asia and Europe than in Africa. African women in antiquity were partners in culture and community. They were more than objects and ornamentation. They have few equals in the minds and imagination of Europeans and Asians.[1]

Herodotus was surprised at African society around 450 B.C.E. He saw women visible in the market and working at trade. Men as well as women were weavers. Nearly a half-century later, Diodorus was surprised that Egyptians did not practice infanticide. They often rescued children left to die by Greek families living in Egypt. He was also surprised that women experienced equality with men. He mistook that equality as female dominance.

African society in antiquity did not view or treat women as helpless, emotional, and inferior appendages while viewing men as strong, adventuresome, and aggressive superiors. The African woman was not silent, secluded, or suppressed. African traditions in many areas appear to have developed a holistic approach to social organization, where both genders were vital participants, partners, and peers.[2]

Traditional African communities were often well-established systems of complementary roles between men and women. Men and women worked side by side in their respective groups, communities, associations, or councils. Men were rulers, warriors, religious leaders, educators, and kingdom builders. Their role and status did not eliminate or exclude women but included their gifts, talents, and influence.

It is interesting to note the perception of the African woman as opposed to the perceptions of women in Greek, Roman, and Jewish thought. The ancient African woman emerges as a full partner with men in civilization building. She is woman, the divine equal of man. She is a daughter, with dual commitments in the village of her birth as *"Ump Add"* (Daughter of the Soil) and in the village of her marriage. She is a wife—a noble and respected role in the family, community, and society, complementary to that of a husband. And she is a mother, respected as the source of life and a vital part of the family's economy, peace, and well-being.[3]

The African woman was not viewed as the secluded and quiet object of history. Reproduction made her a source of life. She was not viewed as the instrument through which evil or death came into the world. She was not considered the weaker-lesser vessel needing to be protected behind veils and drawn curtains hidden from public view.

The status of a woman in the Yoruba tradition was not dependent on the status of her husband. Her place in her social club or market guild primarily determined her status.[4]

In the Roman empire, the names of the female children either had the feminine form of the father's name or a number. In case of divorce, the children belonged to the husband. Among the Suku people of the Southwest Congo, children carried the last name of their mother's family, and they lived in the village of their father's family. At the parents' death, the children belonged to the matrilineal line of their female forebears.[5]

African cave art depicts women not only in maternal and domestic roles, but as warriors with weapons and artisans playing drums and making pottery. Women were pictured as community and ritual leaders.[6] The African woman's place was wherever her gifts would take her.

She had a role in the home with her family, leading great armies, settling disputes, and in the world of commerce and trade.

The ego of the ancient African male was not so fragile that women were discouraged from developing their own talent. Men and women developed a secure community, where both could advance as far as their creative talent could take them.[7]

Some scholars believe that only after years of indoctrination, forced education, and oppression by Asian, Arab, and Western European male-dominated cultures did un-African philosophies and ideologies prevail. The original and authentic African egalitarian structure was discredited. The original traditions were deserted or dropped to embrace civilization.[8]

Not only Africans' imaginations were captured by the Black woman; her presence was felt around the world. Black African women were featured prominently in Greek and Roman mythology. The legendary Greek hero Perseus marries Andromeda, an Ethiopian princess. Grecian vases depict Circe in Homer's *Odyssey* as a Black woman. She was a magician and enchantress in the Greek classic. Circe's niece, Medea, also plays a prominent role in the Odyssey. This daughter of the Colchian king, Aeëtes, helps Jason in his quest for the golden fleece by using her power.[9] The Greek goddess of chastity, Artemis, is African. Also, Minerva, the goddess of wisdom, is an African princess.

Some historians, such as Eloise McKinley-Johnson, believe that the Madonna-and-child pictures and statues by early Christians were patterned after the African goddess Isis suckling her son-god Horus. Several Black Madonnas survive in France, Poland, Switzerland, and Russia. A seventh-century French carving displays a Black Madonna and child with prominent African features.

Ancient Egyptians viewed their queens as the incarnation of Isis. This is a part of their creation of the concept of royalty's divine right. This thought expanded their influence internationally.[10]

Larry Williams and Charles S. Finch write in "The Great Queens of Ethiopia" that the matriarchy probably evolved first in Africa. Even as other social organizations began to replace the older forms, matriarchy continued to thrive, in whole or in part, to the present day. An example of this would be the matrilineal inheritance of the Abiriba of Nigeria, the Akan of Ghana,[11] and of the Egyptian throne during the acknowledged patriarchy of the dynastic period.

The Sukus shared leadership in the family in what Oba T'Shaka describes as "male-female complementarity." The men exercised authority on a daily basis, and the matrilineal system prevailed in matters of inheritance and in legal or policy issues.[12] Among the Jibs of Uganda, the wife's land passes to her daughter at death, not her son. If the daughter has gone to live in the village of her husband, the land then is passed to the wife of the son. In a similar vein, the ownership of the cattle passes from father to son. This is not an act to exercise superiority or inferiority of one gender over another. This is a means to strengthen equal bonds of empowerment and commitment.[13]

Diedre Wimby strongly insists that consanguinity has nothing to do with matriarchy. It was simply an arrangement whereby blood relations would marry to assure the integrity of the blood line.[14] The corpse of a married woman, in some African cultures, would be taken back to the village of her birth. This was done more to emphasize the unbreakable relational bond between her and her ancestral home than to reflect a matriarchal philosophy.[15]

NEFERTITI

African women of antiquity did have their struggles for authority, achievement, and equality. The ancient African woman competed for power and position. She struggled against new ideologies such as patriarchy and materialistic theories, which viewed women as luxuries and objects of civilization, not participants in it.[16] She may have enjoyed popularity and support from community members as well as other leaders. But in some cases, animosity and hatred for her leadership resulted in her image and historical record being destroyed.

This was true of Nefertiti. The wife of Amunhotep IV, known for her beauty and intellect, was not a subservient royal wife. She played an active role in reshaping Black Egypt between 1365 and 1352 B.C.E.

The queen made homages to the god Aeon (Anon) without her husband or with one of her six daughters. She was also pictured leading a major ritual with her husband. She began to be viewed as the divine female partner of her husband, as one who had a right to worship the sun-god without a man as a mediator. This promoted the image and idea that women could bypass the male priesthood to worship their god. The mediator then became the queen, a mother-goddess.[17] This thought—of bypassing a male priest to worship a god—was unacceptable, as it is even now in some religious traditions.

Many of the artistic and sculptural images of Nefertiti were disfigured or destroyed following the death of her husband. Her name and contributions to the reign were diminished.

Nefertiti's husband had broken with the matrilineal tradition by not marrying one of Pharaoh's daughters. Usually, the royal wife was the king's sister or half-sister; she was neither. Amunhotep III, her father-in-law, also had broken with tradition by marrying a commoner, a Nubian-Kushite, Tiye.

TIYE

Tiye is described as having dark brown skin, full lips, full nostrils, and high cheekbones. She reigned as consort and queen mother of Egypt for fifty years.

She was seen to be important not only as the mother of pharaohs Tutankhamen and Akhenaten (Amenhotep IV), but in other roles as well. Tiye coordinated state policies for her husband during his failing health. She also served as secretary of state for her son Akhenaten and his wife, Nefertiti, when they concentrated on religious reform. In the massive statues erected to honor them, Tiye's husband insisted that she be depicted as equal in size to the other rulers—over the objections of the priests, who wanted the queen to be shown as only knee-high to the king.

AHMOS NEFERTERE

During the dynastic period of Egyptian history, Queen Nitocris built the third pyramid at Giza. Queens Tetisheri and Ahmos Nefertere were instrumental in the revolutionary fight against the Hykos.

After the Hykos were driven out, Queen Ahmos Nefertere helped her husband rebuild Kemet. She organized a massive assemblage of field workers to help rebuild the city of the dead at Deir-el-Medina. She was also a religious leader, a high priestess of Amon. Queen Ahmos Nefertere was the first to hold the title of "divine wife." She had a retinue of officials including a majordomo, a chief of troops, and scribes. This queen also had a college of priestesses.[18]

HATSHEPUT

Many Egyptian queens gained their power from their husbands. The exception was Hatsheput. At the death of her husband, Thutmose II, Hatsheput became queen regent for the six-year-old pharaoh, Thutmose III. In the second year of this joint reign, she took full control of the throne.

She ruled Upper and Lower Egypt, Nubia-Kush, and Palestine in the fifth century B.C.E. The two previous warrior pharaohs had led conquering armies out of Egypt up the Euphrates River. She led commercial and trade expeditions. She stabilized Egypt during a season of peace for more than twenty years.

Hatsheput established a new style in female leadership. She wore male clothes, full pharaonic regalia, and added a beard that was held on by a strap. Subjects did not address her with the usual honorifics as "Her Majesty the Queen" but rather as "Her Majesty the King."[19]

NZINGA

In 1623, Nzinga become queen of Ndongo (Angola) and followed the lead of Hatsheput, requiring her subjects to call her "king" and dressing as a man. This queen kept a "harem" of men. Even though there was a council of elders, it was clear to Dutch observers that she was the military strategist of Ndongo. At the age of sixty, she was still leading her warriors into battle.

Nzinga is described as having both the hardness of masculinity and the softness of femininity. She used both readily as she saw fit.[20] Nzinga fought the Portuguese throughout her reign. She is credited with being the first to inspire west central African nationalism.

Joan of Arc was another female leader pictured in male images. She sported short hair and male battle dress. First-century writers also note that Thecla, a missionary disciple who traveled with Paul, cut her hair like a man and wore men's clothing.

Hatsheput, Nzinga, Joan of Arc, and Thecla appear to be women who saw the need to deny their femininity in order to function in authoritative leadership roles. This historical precedent is carried out today by women who feel they too must deny or hide their femininity in leadership positions—especially in male dominated vocations—to gain entrance, credibility, and respect.

One way in which some women claimed equality with men during the early centuries of the developing Christian church, was by transcending gender. The natural physiological function of the female body denied women access to membership and to participation in authoritative leadership roles. Women, by virtue of their menses or natural roles, were excluded from the minyan, the quorum necessary to have worship in the Jewish tradition. Women were excluded from temple activities during menstruation and for a time following childbirth. Therefore, in order to function as leaders, many women and men felt they had to deny their sexual roles through virginity and celibacy, and by adapting their wardrobe or hairstyles to assume the external appearance of the gender in power.[21]

CANDACES

The legacy of African female leadership continued in a line of independent female rulers called Candaces (Kantake) of Ethiopia during the Meroic period (1000 B.C.E.–1000 C.E.). The Candaces produced exceptional palaces, tombs, statues, and other edifices.

They were also warrior queens. Notable among them was Amanirenas. She successfully kept the Roman army out of Nubia when Augustus Caesar occupied Egypt.

Another of the most famous Candaces was Makeda. In southern Arab traditions she is known as Belkis. She is portrayed as the unnamed biblical Queen of Sheba, who journeys to visit King Solomon in the Deuteronomic account in 1 Kings 10. According to some scholars, she captured the heart of King Solomon.[22] Jesus mentioned her as the queen of the South (Matt. 12:42; Luke 11:13). Other nonbiblical writers, such as the Jewish historian Josephus, also wrote of her as the queen of Egypt and Ethiopia.

Makeda served for fifty years, and her reign was said to be one of wisdom, justice, and fortitude. Although scholars debate exactly where Sheba was located, her empire possibly covered Ethiopia, sections of Arabia, Armenia, Syria, India, and Upper Egypt.

Different interpretations by Jewish, Arab, Ethiopian, and other groups have grown up around this visit of the Queen of Sheba or Makeda to King Solomon. The Ethiopians believe that she bore King Solomon a child after the infamous visit. The child was named Menelik. This supposedly began the Solomid line of Ethiopian kings, which continued down to the twentieth-century Haile Selassie. This connection is stated in Article II of the 1955 Ethiopian constitution.[23]

Other scholars view the visit between rulers as something more than a love affair or platonic encounter between rulers. The Queen of Sheba did not leave her massive nation and travel hundreds of miles out of curiosity. She visited King Solomon to organize a trade network, conduct commercial exchange, and settle diplomatic concerns during her stay.[24]

HOMILIA

Hypatia was known as one of the last great woman scientists of antiquity.[25] She wrote and taught on several subjects including mathematics, physics, and astronomy at the University of Alexandria, where she held a chair in philosophy.

Queen Amina of the northern state of Zaria, in the latter part of the fifteenth century, was a progenitor of Hausaland.[26] Queen Dauranama of the neighboring state of Katsina also helped lead the fight for unity of the seven Hausa states, organizing men and women alike.

The Egbe Iyalode was an organization of women in Ibadan and other Yoruba communities. The women were buyers, sellers, and producers who had great impact upon their community and government. These leaders were consulted on political and economic affairs. The leader of the "First Ladies" organization was a member of the (Nigerian) council of state up to 1914.[27]

There are many examples of female leadership in subsequent centuries: Helena and Sabla Wangel of fifteenth-century Ethiopia; Dona Beatrice of Kongo, 1685–1706; Mmanthatisi of Sotho, 1782–1835; Ranavalona I of Madagascar, 1817–1882; Yaa Asantewa of Asante, 1860–1921; and Mehanda of Zimbabwe, 1863–1898.

Queen Ogogo of Umuopara in Umuahia, at the turn of the eighteenth century, led her people's delegation to meet the first British district officer of the Abia state. Later, in 1929, the women led an uprising when rights were denied by the British colonial government. It was called the Aba Women's Riot.[28]

Winnie Mandela continues in the rich legacy of African women who suffer, sacrifice, and provide leadership. She fought against South African apartheid in the spirit of Nzinga, a queen who refused to quit.

These female African leaders—with a wealth of experience in politics, education, government, and religion—represent historical models of particular interest to African American women, who often have had to glean leadership information from other ethnic and gender resources. There is thirst-quenching satisfaction in drawing from one's own artesian well of leadership legacy.

Chapter three

HISTORICAL PERSPECTIVES ON FEMALE LEADERSHIP IN THE CHURCH

"Phoebe, a deacon of the church at Cenchreae . . ." (Rom. 16:1)

The epitome of the "yes, but . . ." tension in the historical perspective between the ideal silent and submissive patriarchal role of women and the individual achievements of female leaders is seen in the growth and development of the church in the United States. Women were the products of a society steeped in hierarchical social and gender stereotypes. They focused most of their attention on the responsibilities of home and family—which is not to say that this was not a worthy or worthwhile emphasis.

"Yes, but . . ." there were women, both in the pew and the pulpit, who also exercised prophetic and pastoral leadership. These women served, for the most part, without benefit of official denominational support: without ordination, appointments, elections, or titles. Yet they founded denominations, started churches, led Bible studies, preached, pastored, evangelized, and served at the head of "women-only" organizations such as missionary societies and parachurch organizations.

It was amazing that women heard the call to preach through the "sounding brass and tinkling cymbals" of cultural biases, traditions, and sexism. The road was not easy and the burdens were not light for many paradigm-pioneering women who faced harsh criticism, rejection, isolation, and even excommunication. Some were even threatened with bodily harm.

Every imaginable argument was used to deny what God had spoken into their hearts. The Bible, which gave them images of women with "like passions," such as Deborah, Huldah, Mary Magdalene, and

Phoebe, was used against them. Biblical interpreters labeled them, among other things, as heretics. Female leaders still responded to the call and made significant leadership contributions to the growth and maintenance of American religious institutions, both from the pulpit and the pew.

THE EIGHTEENTH AND NINETEENTH CENTURIES

It appears that from the earliest colonial times women were organizing, preaching, and/or exercising leadership in religious societies. Several women helped the new American churches with financial support. Women performed functions in the fledgling groups, ignoring gender biases. This included founding churches, evangelizing, and pastoring churches when their husbands died.[1]

The religious beliefs of some women, such as Mary Baker Eddy, led to the establishment of whole movements. The National Christian Scientist Association was founded in 1886 to bring together Eddy followers, who believed that spirituality and positive thinking achieved good health and well-being.[2]

Sally Parsons, Mary Savage, and Clarissa Danforth were prolific itinerant preachers in the Freewill Baptist tradition in the 1790s and early 1800s. In spite of the many churches helped and hundreds of converts, all three remained unordained.

MARGARET FELL

Margaret Fell, called the "Mother of the Society of Friends," instituted the Quaker's "women's meeting." This gave Quaker women, unlike women of other denominations, the opportunity to preach publicly. They also had a voice in the internal management of the ministry and an official role within the administration of the denomination. They supervised marriages, the payment of tithes, the placement of orphans, projects for unemployed women, and the administration of funds for relief programs.

As the fledgling republic began to organize, many colonial churches broke ties with their parent structures in England and elsewhere in Europe. They reorganized as independent "national" bodies, bringing order to practices unregulated during the colonial period.[3]

ANNE HUTCHINSON

Anne Hutchinson (1591–1643) came to the Massachusetts Bay Colony with her husband, William, in 1634. She believed along with her spiritual leader, John Cotton, that not the demonstration of worldly success but a work of God's grace determined an individual's prospect for eternal life. Hutchinson gained a visible role in the community and attracted followers. They met in her home to discuss the earlier week's sermons.

Hutchinson was brought to trial and excommunicated from the colony in 1637. Her major offense was that she was more than a follower of God: she was a religious leader who shared revelations from God in a mixed assembly of men and women. Her actions challenged the belief that women were not able to interpret scripture and share it publicly. She also was accused of witchcraft but never formally tried. She later moved to Rhode Island and was killed with her family in an Indian raid near Long Island Sound.

SARAH OSBORNE

Sarah Osborne (1714–1796) conducted revivals from 1760 to 1796 near her home in Newport, Rhode Island. She authored *Nature and Certainty and Evidence of True Christianity* (1755). In 1741, Osborne founded a prayer society which met faithfully until her death in 1796. Men and women by the hundreds flocked to her home for weekly religious meetings. As her ministry expanded from leading women's prayer groups to leading revivals, Osborne met with opposition from other clergy.

MISSIONARIES

The nineteenth century witnessed the rise of laywoman leaders in the Protestant church movement. Women initially organized within their denominational groups, forming groups for prayer Bible study, mutual aid societies, altar guilds, and missionary societies. These were groups like Anne Hutchinson's which challenged patriarchal paradigms to campaign for the rights of women. These groups could be viewed as the forerunners of various modern denominational commissions on women's issues.

Women then organized outside of the church, focusing on issues such as temperance and abolition. They demonstrated great ability in raising large sums of money to support their work and in networking with other religious groups. Many of these organizations grew into regional and national societies.

In order for women to participate fully in the religious life of their churches, they often formed "women-only" groups, for both White and African American women. They included groups such as the Women's Home and Foreign Missionary Society (A.M.E. Church), Colored Female Religious and Moral Society, Female Mite Society, the Female Religious Biography and Reading Societies, and the Women's Union Missionary Society of America—an interdenominational group which ran hospitals, schools, and orphanages.

These "women-only" clubs gave women an opportunity to participate more fully in the work of their religious traditions, expressing ministerial gifts and leadership within the patriarchal paradigm. These organizations are analogous to the Roman "woman-only" cults, the Hebrew Ladies Relief Society (1871), the Hebrew Ladies Sewing Circle (1869), and the National Council of Jewish Women (1893).

The first professional leadership roles for laywomen in the Protestant tradition in the United States were as missionaries and deaconesses. Missionaries were sent to work both at home and abroad. In many cases, the "assistant missionaries," who were female, outnumbered the ordained male missionaries.[4] By the late 1800s, one thousand missionaries had been dispatched by thirty-three foreign women's missionary societies, the majority being trained in 140 deaconesses' homes.[5]

PROFESSIONAL LAY LEADERS

Catholic nuns were independent professionals. They were educated and self-supporting religious women. Women were not ordained into the priesthood, but they could exercise leadership in the denomination as nuns. They owned and managed property that included schools, convents, farms, orphanages, homes for special groups of people, and hospitals. The nuns achieved all of this while being totally committed to the needs of others, often under the strict authority of men.

Elizabeth Seaton founded a school for girls in Baltimore in 1806.

She later founded the Sisters of Charity of Emmitsburg, Maryland, as the first religious congregation for women in the United States in 1808. There were twelve such groups established between 1790 and 1830, with another 106 by 1900.

In 1811, under the leadership of Mary Rhodes, the Sisters of Loretto in Bardstown, Kentucky, founded a school in a log cabin. By 1812 they had fully established themselves as an order of nuns. They eventually opened schools in six states, and by 1920 they were operating one hundred schools, including two four-year colleges and one junior college. There was a short-lived effort among the Sisters of Loretto to establish an auxiliary religious congregation of Black nuns. Three Black women made the attempt in 1824.

The first permanent community of nuns of African descent, however, were the Oblate Sisters of Providence in Baltimore. The order was founded on July 2, 1829, by four Caribbean women: Rosine Boegues, Mary Frances Balas, Mary Theresa Duchemin, and Elizabeth Lange. They opened their first school in 1843, and the order established Providence Junior College in 1952.[6]

ELIZABETH CADY STANTON

Women such as Sara Crosby, Mary B. Fletcher, Hannah Ball, and Sarah Bently worked diligently with John Wesley, the Father of American Methodism. They carried on revivals and prayer meetings and ministered to the sick and confined. The first organized Methodist churches in the United States and Canada were initiated by the efforts of a woman, Barbara R. Heck (1734–1804). Her family's African American servant was a member of the New York City congregation.

Lucretia Mott (1793–1880), a minister with the Society of Friends, and Elizabeth Cady Stanton were active not only in their denominations but in the abolitionist movements of the nineteenth century. Stanton was converted under the ministry of Charles G. Finney, who outlined in a controversial 1835 lecture his belief that women should be allowed to pray and testify publicly. By 1848, Mott and Stanton organized the first convention on women's rights in New York.

Stanton was known to criticize established religious bodies for their patriarchal view of women. In 1895, she published the first of a two-volume set of *The Women's Bible*. It closely examined various passages of scripture used against women to keep them from leadership positions.[7]

ANTOINETTE BROWN BLACKWELL

Charles Finney became president of Oberlin College in 1835. Pauline Kellogg Wright assumed both the pastorate of the Second Free Presbyterian Church in New York and a professorship in theology at Oberlin possibly as early as 1854. In that same year, the Wesleyan Methodist Church, which was separate from the Methodist Episcopal Church, ordained one of Finney's students, Antoinette Brown (later Blackwell). She is believed to have been the first woman ordained in this country.

In 1853, at the age of twenty-eight, she responded to the call to serve a small Congregationalist church in South Butler, New York. She was ordained a year later. Denomination policy allowed each local church to ordain their own pastors. She served at the church for a few years until ill health forced her to resign.

She married Samuel C. Blackwell in 1856. Brown Blackwell returned to active ministry in the Unitarian tradition. She authored several books in science and philosophy.

Olympia Brown was the first woman ordained by denominational sanction. She was ordained in June 1863 in the Universalist denomination, serving congregations in Bridgeport, Connecticut, and Weymouth, Massachusetts. She graduated from Antioch College in 1860 and pursued graduate study at Canton Theological School.

The first woman ordained in the Methodist Protestant Church was Anna Howard Shaw in 1880. After serving for seven years, she left the pastorate to work for women's suffrage and temperance. She also served for eleven years as president of the National American Women's Suffrage Association (1904–1915) and earned a medical degree.

HOLINESS MOVEMENT

In the Holiness and subsequent Pentecostal movements, women played significant "official" leadership roles. They traveled extensively as evangelists, pastored local churches, held tent revivals and camp meetings, and founded entire denominations. In many instances, women were ordained as preachers and pastors and set aside as bishops while other denominations were still adjusting to the idea of clergywomen.[8]

Phoebe Palmer

Phoebe Palmer, who has been called "a Mother of the Holiness Movement," published several books about holiness in the 1840s. She and her husband, Walter Palmer, preached sermons at summer camp meetings throughout the northeast, Nova Scotia, and the British Isles.

The Palmers opened their home for religious meetings for nearly sixty years. Men, women, ministers, and bishops came every Tuesday evening for the Promotion of Holiness. They also published a magazine, *Guide to Holiness,* which was read widely all over the world.

Frances Willard

Another follower of Charles Finney was Frances Willard. Like Brown Blackwell, she was influenced by Finney's revivals. Willard grew up in upstate New York with a strong reform and temperance background. She later attended Oberlin College. In 1871 she became the president of Evanston College for Ladies, in Illinois. In 1877 she left and served as an assistant to Dwight L. Moody in Boston, Massachusetts.

Willard was a advocate of women's right both in society and in the church. While serving as corresponding secretary and later president of the national Women's Christian Temperance Unions, she encouraged women preachers, inviting them to preach at WCTU conventions. Like Palmer, Willard wrote an early, strong defense of women preaching the gospel, *Woman in the Pulpit.*[9]

Aimee Semple McPherson was the founder of the International Church of the Foursquare Gospel in 1908. The evangelist often preached in the former Angelus Temple in Los Angeles, California, to five thousand or more people.[10] She was noted for a theatrical style that drew national attention. McPherson was also a broadcast pioneer. She was one of the first radio gospel preachers—male or female.

Florence Campbell experienced the Holy Spirit fire while visiting the renowned Azuza Street Church in California. She later founded the Pentecostal Apostolic Faith movement in Portland, Oregon, in 1907.

Alma White was the organizer of the Pillar of Fire denomination. She also published the *Woman's Chain* magazine. She encouraged political action and women's rights.

Hannah Whitehall Smith published *The Secrets of a Happy Life* in 1875.

Kathryn Kuhlman was born in 1907 and rose in the late 1940s to become one of the leaders in the holiness Pentecostal circle. She was a prolific and powerful healing evangelist. Her ministry crisscrossed the United States, touching the lives of hundreds of thousands of people.

AFRICAN AMERICAN WOMEN IN MINISTRY

Africans were first brought to America in 1619. Not all of them were enslaved, but some came as bond servants, explorers, and artisans. They came with their own African religious orientation. (That is not say that Africans were foreign to a Judeo-Christian tradition [Acts 8:26–40].)

There was no rush to convert Africans to the Christian faith. Nonetheless, there are early indications that African converts were baptized in the Puritan colonies. Africans were converted during the revivals of the First and Second Great Awakenings and were even killed during the witch hunts of the northeast colonies.[11]

Enslaved Africans engaged in Christian worship within and beyond the vision and earshot of their masters and mistresses. Annie Sweitzer, an enslaved woman, was one of the founding members of the first Methodist society in the colonies in 1764 in Frederick County, Maryland.[12] A servant by the name of Betty in 1776 was a charter member of the first Methodist society in New York City, called John Street. Enslaved Africans, freed men, and freed women belonged to St. George's Methodist Episcopal Church in Philadelphia, Pennsylvania, as early as the mid-eighteenth century. A young ordained Methodist freed man, Richard Allen, led the Africans' walkout of St. George's Church in 1786. They left and developed a new denominational thrust, the African Methodist Episcopal Church, not because of theological differences but because of racial injustice.

Just as women of ancient Africa were not silent and subservient, African American women of the eighteenth and nineteenth centuries did not view themselves as fragile or helpless, in the way that the larger society portrayed White women.[13] Our female African ancestors viewed their maternal roles as more than just a paradigm category. They used the role of motherhood as an opportunity to raise, nurture, and train the children who would one day rise up and free "Israel" from the hand of the oppressor.[14]

The social injustices of the era were so catastrophic that women did not see themselves as separate from men but as allies with men. They were willing participants against slavery and later racism, prejudicial laws, Jim Crowism, and other apartheid-like structures. They reinterpreted the roles of mother, sister, daughter, and wife from positions of weakness into positions of power and influence. Biblical images of women serving with men in mission and ministry motivated them into action.[15]

While women looked for men to be allies with them not only against racism but sexism as well, many men did not return the favor. In the development of churches and denominations totally led and controlled by African Americans, sexism reared its ugly head. "Yes, but . . ." women still played critical leadership roles.

The African American church was not exempt from the impetus felt by the increasing leadership roles sought and assumed by African American women. Women, from the earliest times, always constituted a major portion of the congregations. And they emerged to develop effective and efficient parachurch organizations, such as missionary societies and women's mite societies that were significant in the development and maintenance of the local church.

Our foremothers' preaching, seeking ordination, and planting churches represent extraordinary examples of courage and perseverance under fire. These women included Jarena Lee, Rebecca Cox Johnson, Amanda Berry Smith, Zilpha Elaw, Julia A. J. Foote, and an enslaved African named Elizabeth.

ELIZABETH

In the late 1700s, a former enslave African named Elizabeth (no last name was recorded) was a known preacher among the Quakers in Virginia and Maryland. She was born in Maryland in 1766 to enslaved parents, who were both literate and religious. Her family belonged to the Methodist society. Her father read the Bible aloud every Sabbath morning to his family.

Elizabeth began preaching at about the age of thirty. She traveled extensively until her nineties in the Maryland, Virginia , Pennsylvania, and Michigan areas and in Canada, where there were several welcoming settlements of Africans. In Michigan, she founded an orphanage for orphans of color.[16]

Elizabeth preached in areas with established Quaker meetinghouses. She also preached in remote places where there were no meetinghouses and in locations where people opened their homes to her to hold meetings.

In 1796 Virginia authorities stopped her and inquired whether she was ordained. She replied that she was ordained by God and not by the hands of man. Who better than God? It was reported that they let her go.[17]

In 1889 the Quakers published a tract, *Elizabeth, a Colored Minister of the Gospel Born in Slavery*. It contains her own testimony, given at the age of 97. She is said to have lived until age 101, settling among the Quakers in Philadelphia.[18]

JULIA FOOTE

On May 20, 1894, Julia A. Foote, a conference missionary, became the first woman to be ordained a deacon in the African Methodist Episcopal Zion Church. She was ordained an elder in 1900.

Foote was born in 1823 in Schenectady, New York, and grew up with parents who advocated strong Christian beliefs. She married George Foote, a sailor, and moved with him to Boston. There she joined the A.M.E.Z. Church. Foote began to proclaim the gospel to others within and outside of her church, holding evangelistic meetings in her home. At this point, she was read out of the church.

Foote joined other women in Philadelphia to sponsor a series of religious meetings in a hired hall. She presided over the services and over other unofficial religious gathering in upstate New York. In 1845, she began preaching in various pulpits with, in the company of, or invited by A.M.E.Z. ministers. Foote traveled the Mid-Atlantic and New England states preaching. She eventually settled down in 1850 in Cleveland, Ohio.

Foote engaged in ministry while trying to balance the responsibilities of family and home. Her husband was not supportive of her ministry and tried to discourage her. When his efforts could not stop her, he became distant in their marriage.

Many clergywomen can identify with the challenge of balancing the responsibilities of home, work , marriage and ministry. There are women in ministry who can also identify with the agony and pain of nonsupportive spouses and families.

The wife of AMEZ Bishop John B. Small, Mary J. Small in 1895 was the second woman to be ordained a deacon (after Foote). In 1898 she became the first woman ordained an elder.

JARENA LEE

Jarena Lee was born in Cape May, New Jersey, a free African woman. In 1804, she was employed as a house servant in Philadelphia and was influenced by the preaching of the Reverend Richard Allen. She professed a call to the gospel ministry and kept a detailed record of her experiences. This record was later published.

In 1809 she approached Allen, the pastor of Bethel African Methodist Episcopal Church in Philadelphia, Pennsylvania, and requested a license to preach. Allen denied her request, believing at that time that women could hold prayer meetings but not preach.[19]

She was married to Joseph Lee, the pastor of a Methodist society outside of Philadelphia. He died in 1811, leaving her with two children to raise alone. Lee began to preach after the tragic deaths of her husband and four other members of her family. She remained dedicated to the ministry, even though she was often separated from her children. She demonstrated great courage when her ministry put her at odds with men in and out of the church.

She wrote about having a vision in which one day her enemies would become her friends. After the A.M.E. Church was organized as a denomination, the pastor of Bethel A.M.E. Church, the now Bishop Richard Allen, was transformed into a friend. He became supportive of her efforts after hearing her preach one day when a male preacher started to preach and then failed or "lost the spirit." Allen then believed that Lee was called to preach.

Lee traveled over 2,300 miles, delivering 178 sermons in the early 1800s while in her forties. She held prayer meetings and was the first woman to preach in the A.M.E. Church; however, she was never ordained. Not until 1884 were women finally licensed to preach in the A.M.E. Church. Women were not ordained in the denomination until 1948.

Lee's tremendous preaching gift provides an inspiring legacy for African American clergywomen in particular. She models courage, commitment, and dedication in ministry without official recognition, title, or ordained status.

Other committed A.M.E. women, along with Lee, called themselves "the Daughters of the Conference." They were Sylvia Murray, Elizabeth Cole, Harriet Felston Taylor, and Amanda Berry Smith. These women were instrumental in articulating women's gifts, the call to leadership, and ordination within the A.M.E. Church.

AMANDA BERRY SMITH

Amanda Berry Smith was another A.M.E. preacher who served without ordination. Smith was born an enslaved African in 1837 in Long Green, Maryland, just outside the city of Baltimore. Although her parents were enslaved, living on adjoining farms, they were literate. They saw that young Amanda could read by the age of eight and went to a private school during the summer months.[20]

Her father worked long hours after the day's work, making brooms and husk mats to sell. He later was able to purchase his own freedom and that of his wife and five children. The young evangelist-to-be grew up in a strong family characterized by literacy and faith in God.[21] She later married a local deacon of a Methodist Episcopal Church, who abandoned her. Her second husband died, and she supported herself as a washerwoman.

After the Civil War, Smith acknowledged her call to preach, not in the A.M.E. Church but with the Holiness movement. Her ministry initially began at a national Holiness camp meeting in Maryland during the revivals of the 1860s and 1870s. She traveled throughout the United States and Great Britain, preaching at Holiness camp meetings.

She later left the country in 1878 and spent fourteen years evangelizing in England. This led to work with Bishop J. M. Thoburn of Calcutta, India, and also to evangelistic crusades and missionary work in Africa. All of this was done without ordination. She felt that her ordination was by God and that humankind did not need to affirm what had already been done.

Smith was not only a powerful preacher of the gospel but also was gifted with a tremendous singing voice. Her voice and messages brought considerable attention and respect.

Smith modeled the leadership qualities of tact and diplomacy for the "Daughters of the Conference" who followed her. Members of the Plymouth brethren opposed her, publishing opposition stories about her and trying to draw her into a public debate. Smith politely refused, continuing her preaching mission. They were in opposition because Smith was a woman, not because she was African American.

In 1890 Smith retired in Chicago and started an orphanage. She remained active in Holiness circles until her death in 1915.

ZILPHA ELAW

Zilpha Elaw was an evangelist and missionary who was a contemporary of Jarena Lee. The two shared a pulpit at one time. Like Lee, Elaw was born a freed woman.

Elaw distinguished herself as a missionary. She traveled extensively and, like Lee, demonstrated exceptional courage. She traveled to slave states in the late 1820s, risking arrest, kidnapping, or sale into bondage. She later opened a school in Burlington, New Jersey. In 1840, Elaw began her preaching ministry. She preached not only in the United States but in England, encountering recurring opposition.

Elaw writes in her *Memoirs* that in Burlington, New Jersey, the ministers of the Methodist Society were receptive to an African American woman preaching. This group endorsed her "call" to the gospel ministry. Many persons—African American, White, male, and female—came to her "pulpit debut." Initially, however, the other African American ministers gave her a cool reception.

REBECCA COX JACKSON

Rebecca Cox Jackson, the sister of an A.M.E. minister, also faced rejection when announcing her call to preach. She later left the denomination and established an African American Shaker community.

These eighteenth and nineteenth century African American women responded to the call to the ministry without official ordination and were often unlicensed. They were ignored or were unrecognized by their denominations, but not by the people whose lives they touched. Many of them were forced to start their own independent churches, join new developing denominations, or submit to secondary leadership roles.

Several denominations did begin to ordain women by the late 1800s. They are the African Methodist Episcopal Zion Church (1894), the American Baptist Churches (1800), the Christian Church (Disciples of Christ [1888]), and the United Brethren in Christ (1889).

Churches of the Cumberland Presbyterian Church were ordaining women as ruling elders in the late 1880s and 1890s. In 1889, Louisa Woolsely was ordained to a ministry of word and sacrament.[22] Not until the twentieth century would the larger Presbyterian Church in the U.S.A. in the North (1955) and the Presbyterian Church in the U.S. in the South (1964) ordain woman as ministers.[23]

THE TWENTIETH CENTURY

Women expressing a call to the gospel ministry still had to follow a path strewn with rejection, skepticism, struggle, and doubt, in spite of increased opportunities for ministry training and ordination. The official rules regarding clergywomen were changed, but the unofficial traditions concerning "male-only" leadership positions remained the same. The unofficial traditions still held that only men could serve as pastors, presiding elders, ruling elders, district superintendents, denominational heads, or bishops.

Women were often ordained into the ministry and just tolerated. They were offered little or no assistance. It was not unusual for women to be stranded to navigate the passageways of ministry alone. The idea that a sovereign God might choose the son of a harlot (Judg. 11:1), a shepherd boy (1 Sam. 16:13), an ass (Num. 22:21–30), and women (Judg. 4–5; John 4; Rom. 16:1) may be good in discussion, church discipline, or theory. But praxis is another thing.

There were doubts about the capacity of women and their suitability for pastoral care. There were doubts about whether women could administer and command the respect of a community. There were concerns about how a woman would handle natural physiological changes, such as pregnancies and menopause. There was still skepticism about whether women could preach a weekly schedule, manage a pastorate and a family without either one suffering.

Pregnancy brings home the issue of a pastor's femininity. Pregnancy cannot be hid by clergy robes, nor can swelling feet, finicky appetite, and morning sickness. Yet many women successfully juggle numerous responsibilities such as pregnancy, home, and church. In 1985, while the pastor of a circuit—two churches, Bethel and Ebenezer AME Churches in Cecil County, Maryland—I became pregnant with our third child. (My husband, Stan, and I had been married for seventeen years, and this was my second year in the pastorate.) God blessed me to pastor my church, managing a full teaching and preaching schedule, right up to my due date—including nine hours of seminary courses, a four-hour on-air shift at WEBB radio, duties at home, and my sanity. Joi-Marie Murphy McKenzie was born Sunday, October 13, 1985, five hours after Sunday morning worship, not without a struggle. In two weeks, I was back in church. In another week, I was preaching again. My able associate, Rev. Bernice Givens, fulfilled all the other responsibilities and commitments until I was at full strength. If a male pastor had had major surgery, an associate, if one was available, or another minister would carry the weight of the congregation until the pastor returned.

These concerns were widely held by male clergy and the laity, both men and women. In fact, one of the perennial arguments against female pastors is that it is not the men of the church who object but the women who do not want a woman in the pulpit! Critics of women in the ministry enjoy this excuse.

Why don't women want other women in the pulpit? Some believe that the pulpit is historically one of the few places African American men can exert strong, positive leadership, and for that reason African American women should let them do so. Others feel the pulpit is one of the few remaining positions where women can interact with men who are sensitive to their spiritual needs. The pulpit can produce a man who is willing to direct women's spiritual growth and development, and is attentive and responsive to them in a crisis. He models behavior that is valued and appreciated.

Others would even go so far as to say that the only hug, compliment, or encouragement some women receive all week comes from their male pastor. Still others believe that some women have problems working with other women. None of the reasons shared during the Women Surviving in Ministry seminar had anything to do with theological or biblical perspectives.

Often women don't want other women in the pulpit simply because this represents a change in tradition neither articulated nor supported by authorizing bodies. Perhaps there would be a different attitude if these bodies took the same care in introducing female leadership to congregations as they do in introducing a new denominational thrust, stewardship drive, or liturgy.

Nevertheless, women continued to enter the ministry in increasing numbers. It was "by their fruits" (Matt. 7:20) along with talent, competence, and surviving power that silenced many of the naysayers.

Mary L. Tate is credited with founding the Church of the Living God, the Pillar, and the Ground of Truth Church in 1908. It is believed that Mother Leafy Anderson established the Church of the Redemption in Chicago in 1915. She later moved to New Orleans to start the Eternal Life Spiritual Church around 1918–21.[24]

Laura J. Lang became in 1936 the first woman ordained a local elder in the Lexington Conference of the Methodist Episcopal Church. In 1956, Salle A. Crenshaw, an African American woman, became the first to be admitted to full connection, granted Annual Conference membership, and ordained.[25]

In the Episcopal Church, Phyllis Edwards was "recognized" by Bishop James Pike as a deacon, utilizing her deaconess ordination in 1965. Eleven female deacons were ordained into the priesthood in an "irregular" ordination in Philadelphia on July 20, 1974, by two retired bishops and one resigned bishop in the presence of a presiding or diocesan bishop. In the next two years, the church was in turmoil, grappling with the issue of the unauthorized ordination. Finally, in September 1976, the General Convention approved of the 1974 ordination of the eleven women and approved the ordination of women into the priesthood and into the episcopacy.

The Reverend Pauli Murray became the first African American woman ordained an episcopal priest on January 8, 1977. Fifty-eight-year-old African American priest Barbara C. Harris on February 11, 1984, became the first woman consecrated a bishop in the worldwide Anglican communion. She was consecrated Bishop Suffragant, meaning she held administrative responsibilities and was not in charge of a diocese. In October 1983, the third female American consecrated an Episcopal bishop was assigned to head the Diocese of Vermont.

In 1955, Mrs. Sheldon Robbins became the first female cantor in Judaism. By the late 1960s, the Hebrew Union College began to admit women to study to become rabbis. Sally Priesand graduated in 1972 and became the first female rabbi (Reform) in the United States.[26]

Sandy Eisenberg (Sasso) became the first woman rabbi in 1974 in the Reconstructionist movement. The first woman rabbi in Conservative Judaism was Amy Eilbery in 1985. In 1994, Laura Geller was named senior rabbi for Temple Emmanuel in Beverly Hills, California, a major metropolitan Jewish congregation.

In the Presbyterian tradition, Thelma Davidson Adair was the first African American moderator in the United Presbyterian Church. In the same year, Sara Brown Cordery became the first African American woman to become the moderator of the Baltimore Presbytery.

Denise Page Hood was the first African American female to chair the Executive Council of the United Church of Christ in 1968. Dr. Cynthia L. Hale became the first woman to head the National Convocation of the Christian Church (Disciples of Christ) in 1982. She is the founder and pastor of Ray of Hope Christ Church (Disciples of Christ) in Atlanta, Georgia. There are more than eight hundred members in this fast-growing African American congregation.

Dr. Suzan D. Johnson Cook was the first female and first African American to pastor a church in the American Baptist Church in the U.S.A. Mariner's Temple Baptist Church in New York City is a growing and thriving church of more than seven hundred members. The Wednesday noon service hosts five hundred worshipers weekly. Dr. Johnson Cook occupies several roles. She is pastor, visiting professor of homiletics at Harvard Divinity School, author of several books, wife, and mother of two children.

The Catholic Church still prohibits women from serving as priests. The Church of God in Christ prohibits women from serving as pastors but recognizes them to serve as missionaries and evangelists.

Several women have navigated the political waters of major denominations to serve as bishops. There are women who have been serving as bishops of independent churches, mostly on the East Coast, for several decades. Among them are Bishop Ida B. Robinson, the founder of the Mt. Sinai Holy Church, established in 1924.

Marjorie Matthews in 1980 was consecrated the first female bishop of a major denomination in the United States, the United Methodist Church. The first African American female to be elevated to the bishopric of a large denomination was the Reverend Leontine J. Kelly. She was elected and then consecrated on July 20, 1984, in the United Methodist Church.

"I don't think we need to spend quality time to defend our call," stated Bishop Leontine Kelly in a recent interview in Chicago. "Those who are called, just do it. . . . I really didn't have too much difficulty as long as I kept my place," she continued. "It wasn't until I ran for bishop that I experienced most of my problems." (Bishops are elected regionally in the United Methodist tradition.)

"We learned that we really had to organize as women. We must continue to help each other. We must network with other racially ethnic women, form support groups, keep in touch by mail if you have to, but we must stay connected."

She endured the "heat" of the campaign "to confront and combat." "We as Black women bear the brunt of the whole thing. That is why my running was a dual confrontation: for women and for Black America."

She believes that women still face many challenges: "Women have to see that they must keep opening doors in the church and society if things are going to change," she concluded.

Five women have been elected bishops in the United Methodist Church. They include Bishop Marjorie S. Matthews, Bishop Judith Craig, Bishop Sharon Brown Christopher, Bishop Susan M. Morrison, and Bishop Kelly, retired.

One of the first African American clergywoman appointed as district superintendent in the United Methodist Church was the Reverend Charlotte Nichols. Following closely behind was the Reverend Mary Brown Oliver, who served as district superintendent in the Baltimore-Washington Annual Conference. Oliver was appointed to that administrative position after leading the 548-member Northwood-Appold United Methodist Church in Baltimore, Maryland, from 1988 to 1990. Howard University honored her in 1991 with a Trailblazer Award for achievement.

In the African Methodist Episcopal Church, four women have been appointed to serve in similar middle-management positions, as presiding elders. They are the Reverend Ernestine Ward, presiding elder of the Buffalo-Ibant District in New York. In 1988 she became the first woman to be appointed into that position. Reverend Ida Keener, presiding elder of the Brenham District in the West Texas Annual Conference, was appointed in 1990. The Reverend Olive E. Moses was appointed in 1992 as presiding elder over the Provincial District in Freetown, Sierra Leone, West Africa. In 1994 Reverend A. A. Pholo was appointed a presiding elder in Lesotho in southern Africa. The Reverend Carolyn Tyler, former pastor of the 600-member Walker Temple A.M.E. Church in Los Angeles, was appointed presiding elder in the Southern California Annual Conference in 1994.

There are a growing number of African American women serving as pastors to congregations of over 600. There are the already-mentioned Dr. Hale and Dr. Johnson Cook; Rev. Johnnie Coleman, Chicago; Dr. Barbara King, Atlanta; Rev. Dorothy Watson Tatem, who serves the 700-member Camphor Memorial United Methodist Church; Rev. Jean Young, former district superintendent, serving the 1,120-member Epworth United Methodist Church in Prince George's County, Maryland; and Dr. Barbara Sands, serving the 600-member Ashbury-Broadneck United Methodist Church. Sands was formerly Associate Director of Church and Community Ministries of the Baltimore Annual Conference of the United Methodist Church and the first woman to be elected president of the prestigious Central Maryland Ecumenical Council.

The majority of African American clergywomen serve excellently and efficiently churches with two hundred or fewer congregants. One of the next challenges to sexism in the church, is for clergywomen to move beyond "first appointment" churches or entry-level positions. Clergywomen face a "glass ceiling" or stained-glass ceiling of their own. The advancement up the denominational ladder is within view, but women have been unable to move in significant numbers beyond the local church to serve in denominational positions and on the episcopal level to effect change and/or be a part of the decision dynamic on the denominational level. Another challenge is to move beyond the tokenism of the "first and only woman" elected or appointed to this, that, or the other office.

Chapter four

THEOLOGICAL PERSPECTIVES SUPPORTING AND REJECTING FEMALE LEADERSHIP

ONE'S PERSPECTIVE IS the lens through which one views and evaluates available information. Ultimately, the commitment to a belief system or course of action is rooted in the convictions developed from that information through a perspective.

There are several perspectives that shape a theological structure for the support or rejection of female leadership in the church. There is the traditional male-articulated arguments that stem from Barth's minimizing human experience and elevating the Word of God alone as the starting point for "doing" theology.[1]

This "universal" theological perspective becomes problematic for liberation theologians and feminist theologians. They contend that the experience out of which Christian theology is formed is not a universal experience but the experience of the dominant culture; the experiences of women, African American men and women, and other oppressed people are not considered.

James Cone in *God of the Oppressed* indicates that although God, the subject of theology, is eternal, those who articulate it are not. The language of theology is limited by history and time. It is not sensitive to the ideas, purposes, and assumptions of a particular group of people. It is not universal.[2]

Feminists, therefore, propose a theology that emerges out of the particular experience of women. Liberationists propose a theological approach out of the experience of oppressed people, and womanist theologians suggest a theology that emerges out of the experience of African American women.

This is why a review of the status of women in Greek, Roman,

Jewish, and African societies was pertinent to this discussion. These societies created a particular historical experience for women which had an impact on the emergence of women as leaders in the community and the church. Contributions deemed marginal by some materialize as significant when contextualized in the experiences of historical and contemporary women. "Women's experiences" are the complex feelings and struggles shared by women in various circumstances of life.[3]

God is generally referred to as the Holy One, Creator, Supreme Being, and other terms that have been historically masculine. The usage of male personal pronouns has been problematic for feminist and womanist theologians. Theology that is synonymous with the masculine experience is insufficient to deal with women's experience.[4] These groups argue for the maleness and femaleness of God.

Womanist theologians such as Jacqueline Grant take it one step further. The ground for "doing" theology must include the experience of African American women. This "ground" is not male-exclusive but inclusive. Many African American women have rejected exclusionary perspectives that would be detrimental to the liberation of African Americans as a whole. This perspective gives African American women the opportunity to be "both/and": African American and African American women, who can be concerned about both racism and sexism.

Concurrently, human history, philosophy, behavioral science, and physical sciences are also exceptional resources for "doing" theology. However, we must look to the Bible as the resource that provides insights not available from any other source.

Dr. Cain Felder argues that the Bible has been distorted through the lens of a Eurocentric hermeneutics. This interpretive stance—which passes for the scholarly norm and standard—is in fact a hermeneutics that is not "objective" but culture-bound. It needs to be challenged by the African American scholarly community.[5]

Therefore, I would argue for a biblical womanist theological perspective. *Womanist* is a term developed by Alice Walker to embody the African American women's experience. It speaks of surviving in the struggle, of being in charge, courageous, assertive, and bodacious. It speaks of being fully grown and responsible enough to contemplate and dialogue theologically independent of other races and gender.[6] *Womanist* bespeaks of the "Daughters of the Conference," Jarena Lee, Amanda Berry Smith, and other contemporary clergywomen who have had to be forthright, courageous, and assertive in order to respond to God's call.

The biblical womanist theological viewpoint recognizes the Bible as an important body of information for the Christian. The Bible remains the major source for African American women to validate and affirm their understanding of a God who directly relates to them and whose Word is perceived within their experiences.[7]

A biblical womanist perspective also considers the experience of African Americans and the African American woman as the ground to begin to develop a reality upon which we can be guided. African American women must develop a conviction that affirms Jesus' revolutionary message as freedom for her as a woman and as an African American woman. This theological perspective emerges out of the African American woman's experience with racism, sexism, and classism.

This chapter will look at the theological perspectives that reject female leadership in the church. It will also examine the perspectives that support women in the ministry, such as feminist, womanist, and liberationist theologies. The chapter will conclude by looking at theological issues facing African American female leaders in the church.

THEOLOGICAL REJECTION OF FEMALE LEADERSHIP IN THE CHURCH

Women were prominent leaders in the early church, up to and after the middle of the second century. They were more than deaconesses concerned with widows and orphans. They were church leaders who taught, debated, healed, and perhaps even baptized.[8]

By the third and fourth centuries, church orders reflected the rejection of female leadership by patriarchal society. The *Didascalia Apostolorum* states that since women were not specifically appointed by Jesus to teach and prophesy, they should not proclaim the Christ. This document notes that there were women who were disciples. However, Jesus would have instructed the others if the women were to teach.[9]

In the *Apostolic Church Order* there is a dialogue indicating a disagreement between female and male disciples about whether or not the women could be celebrants. Other objections to women as the transmitters of the gospel and apostolic tradition are seen in other noncanonical writings such as the Gospel of Mary and the Acts of Paul and Thecla.

Apostolic tradition and revelation are often viewed by the mainstream church as a support to church organization and theology. The Montanists cited the succession of female prophets in the Scriptures to justify prophecy by women. The gnostics also cited female disciples of Christ, such as Mary Magdalene and Salome, while mainstream thought downplayed the role of the women and concentrated on Paul and the twelve apostles.[10]

The debate between Peter, the opponent of gnosis, and Mary Magdalene, the proponent of gnosis, was about whether women had received divine revelation and then could transmit apostolic tradition. The same argument is reflected in debates between the mainstream church and gnosticism; patriarchal and egalitarian Christian groups.[11]

The ascetic movement dominated fourth-century church life. The stringent ascetic life was liberating for many women. Women were not limited by social female roles. They were able to achieve some measure of independence in communities led and directed by women.[12] Many women flocked to the ascetic life communities and exerted leadership functions within their convents. They counted on the support of the church to counter their families' demand of marriage and procreation.

Leaders such as Macrina and Paula looked to Thecla as their ascetic role model. Thecla sacrificed everything, including her love relationships and the security of her family and home, to travel with Paul. Paul designated her an apostle of the gospel.[13]

Patriarchal writers could not totally omit mention of the women who were leaders in the early church. Those women who could not be deleted were give diminished roles. They were also declared as frauds and heretics. Phoebe was reduced to an assistant of Paul by Origen and Chrysostom, who wrote that only when the "angelic" conditions exist can women serve in the leadership positions of disciples or apostles.[14]

The original egalitarian vision of oneness in Christ is clouded by those who attempt to justify exclusive male leadership. The remnant of this tradition reminds us that the faith community was to be one of mutual service.[15] Later opponents to female leadership in the church most frequently cited the advice given by Paul to the church at Corinth, "Let your women keep silence in the churches" (1 Cor. 11:3), and also to Timothy, "Let the women learn in the silence with all subjection" (1 Tim. 2:11).

Paul pronounced that women were to remain silent in church and should not attempt to address the congregation—that is, "to teach or usurp authority over man." The suggestion in the epistle to the church at Corinth is that if women want to learn, to question, or to respond to any activity or ideas within the church, they must do so at home with their husbands. There is a hierarchy that proceeds from God to Christ to man to woman.

One proponent of this argument was Henry Van Dyke. In an article in *The Homiletic Review* in 1888, Van Dyke argued that because only men were chosen to follow Christ, then women would be "eternally" excluded from obtaining any leadership positions within the church. He discounted any reference to the many women who traveled with Christ and overlooked that the first person to carry the news of the resurrected savior was a woman.

Van Dyke did not support a total ban on female leadership in the church. He suggested that women assume no "visible leadership" roles. They could serve in "helpmeet" functions, such as visiting the sick and confined.[16]

There is still much contemporary theological debate about female leadership. Jacquelyn Grant in *White Women's Christ and Black Women's Jesus*, notes that the Catholic Church still rigidly continues to prohibit female leadership, in this case, ordination. The 1977 *Vatican Declaration* contends that only a man as a priest could represent and image the Christ.[17]

In some conservative evangelical thought, the issue of female leadership in the church was settled until women became influenced by cultural changes instigated by the feminist and other liberationist movements. These conservatives believe that Christian tradition and practices hold that women cannot occupy prominent and visible leadership roles, including elder, teacher, or any role that gives them authority over men.[18]

There were women who were disciples, prophets, and deacons. There were no women indicated among the original twelve, but there were also no White Anglo-Saxon males. Jesus told the women at the tomb to go and tell, and the woman at the well led a revival in Sychar. In summary, the theological debate focuses on several objections to female leadership in the church. These objections include such statements as: Christ did not choose women to follow him, women were not apostles, women did not drink from the cup with Christ at the last supper, women were not told specifically and explicitly, "Women, go ye therefore and preach, teach, and pastor."

I have heard other objections from men and women who were members of a church I was serving. One member said that the only real objection she had was that she just could not get used to hearing a woman pray the morning prayer. She was used to a male voice.

Another member, male, could not get used to seeing a woman sit above him in the pulpit. God made man first and placed him over woman. Women are not supposed to exercise authority over men. These objections and others like them stem mostly from issues of power, control, and who is in charge.

Other theological objections center on texts such as the "household codes." The rejection of female leadership then centers on women being categorically subordinate in hierarchy that is supported by Christ, scripture, and the church.

THEOLOGICAL SUPPORT FOR FEMALE LEADERSHIP IN THE CHURCH

> "And it shall come to pass . . . that I will pour out my Spirit upon all flesh; and your sons, and daughters shall prophecy." (Joel 2:28)

Just as some theological perspectives reject female leadership in the church, there are some theological viewpoints that support them. Among these are feminist theology, womanist theology, and liberationist theology. One cannot support female leadership in the church without being considered a feminist, womanist, or liberationist. However, support for female leadership may also rise out of what some consider the egalitarian nature of the New Testament (Gal. 3:28).

Ann Loades describes feminism in *Feminist Theology* as a movement that seeks social justice and political change for women. Feminism can be viewed as a doctrine of social and political rights, an advocate organization seeking justice for women, a theory designed to create an awareness for the necessity of long-term social change.[19]

Loades describes three different types of feminism. The first, "liberal feminism," is concerned with equality of civil rights for women and men. The second, "Marxist feminism," concerns itself with economic autonomy. The third, "Romantic Feminism," promotes emotional and natural aspects rather than technical aspects. Romantic feminism includes radical women who reject the male world and those who seek a partnership with it.[20]

When it comes to the subject of theology, Loades argues that what was thought of as a "universal" theology actually excludes women. No one sex, male or female, should monopolize alleged truths about God. She echoes Gerda Lerner's cry of "Androcentric fallacy," that what has been stated as the whole truth is actually half. It is erroneous to believe that only male experiences and ideas alone represent universal opinion.[21] This fallacy has been built into the mental structures of western civilization and cannot be corrected by adding a few liturgical phrases or appointing women to a few positions. A few cosmetic changes are not sufficient. A total restructuring of thought and analysis that respects both genders is needed.[22]

Dr. Cain Felder raises a similar issue when it comes to Afrocentrism, which he defines as placing Africans and those of African descent as proactive participants within history and/or theology rather than passive subjects of them. Africans and those of African descent become centers of value, neither being diminished nor diminishing any other group.[23] As far as he is concerned, western Eurocentric theology has not done this.

Grant, in *White Women's Christ and Black Women's Jesus*, also argues that theology developed in Europe and America has excluded the majority of humanity. Only when Christology and theology are contextualized do marginalized people, such as women and other oppressed groups, become participants rather than recipients of dogma. As participants, the oppressed are able to dialogue on the gospel for the oppressed.

Another type of feminist is the "liberation feminist," whose primary interest is in the liberation of women and generally of humanity (which may be seen as similar to Loades's liberal feminism). Within that perspective, there are two viewpoints: one defines its position based on scripture and the other uses scripture as one of the sources available for doing theology. The "rejectionist feminist," on the other hand, views neither the scripture nor tradition as valid sources for reflection and doing theology.

An example of the "biblical feminist" response to rejections of female leadership is Denise Lardner Carmody's exegesis, found in *her book Biblical Woman: Contemporary Reflection on Scriptural Texts.* She cites 1 Corinthians 11:3, "But I would have you know, that the head of every man is Christ; and the head of every woman is the man; and the head of Christ is God," and discusses the issue of headship, contending that Jesus promoted an egalitarian community that was in tension with Jewish and Hellenistic culture. The "household codes," among other things, indulged Jewish and Hellenistic social mores so that the members of the emerging Christian faith did not draw undue attention to what some may view as anarchic behavior.[24]

Although not considered biblical feminists, Lawrence O. Richards and Clyde Hoeldtke, in *A Theology of Church Leadership*, assert that a misunderstanding of headship can lead one to believe that it implies position, hierarchy rather than relationship.[25] They assert that Old Testament headship promoted hierarchical lines of authority and responsibility. New Testament headship is organic. In order to understand New Testament headship, the church—which is itself organic—must begin to build its understanding of leadership from the new covenant rather than the old.[26]

There are several scriptural references to which proponents of female leadership in the church point. They include implicit action by women such as the woman at the well, who went to tell her neighbors about Jesus (John 4:28–29), and the women such as Mary, Mary Magdalene, and Salome, who first carried the message about the resurrected Christ (Matt. 28:1; Luke 24:9–10; John 20:17–18).

Women who performed explicit leadership functions included Lydia, in the church in her home; Prisca or Priscilla, who co-pastored with her husband, Aquila; and the four daughters of Philip, who prophesied.

Other scriptural references include the egalitarian call of Galatians 3:28. Carmody writes that the church needs to practice the radical sexual equality found in this passage. The distinctions that qualified a person in the past are now null and void. The new believer is to be viewed in light of the equality shared by all children of God and members of one body of Christ.[27]

There appears to be a need for the New Testament ideals spoken by Jesus and Paul regarding class discriminations, freedom, social, sexual, and ethnic backgrounds to be pushed to the front burner. The urgency is motivated by an increasingly hostile environment to these diversities and persistent institutional social, racial, gender, and class prejudices. Felder notes that there is a need to elevate these ideals again so that they can speak to today's church leadership and laity who refuse to see sexism as a social evil.[28]

The scriptural texts of Galatians 3:28, "There is neither Jew nor Greek, there is neither male nor female: for we are all one in Christ Jesus," as well as Colossians 3:1–11, "But Christ is all, and in all," clearly transform the previous shallow distinctions of race, class, and sexual and social background into a new humanity.[29] A new universalism and unity are expressed as human beings that love God, and love their neighbor as they love themselves.

As one recognizes Christ as the center of this new humanity, the criteria for inclusion such as ritual laws of cleanliness, ethnic origin, or national origin are changed to: "Christ is all, and in all" (Col. 3:11).

It is ironic that in these two pericopes and others, Paul is seen issuing a call for a new humanity, united and reconciled. Paul affirms inclusiveness that does not exclude female leadership. The divisive notions of superiority and inferiority based on class, race, and social and sexual grounds come under attack. They find no validity in Christ. The new criteria are based upon being buried with Christ in baptism and raised up to be a part of the universal brotherhood and sisterhood.

This is ironic because it is this self-same Paul who is used to support the rejection of female leadership. It is as if Paul is portrayed as a "wimp," changing his mind to fit his audience. Or, perhaps he grew egalitarian between 1 Corinthians and Galatians. Or perhaps, later editors projected patriarchal perspectives on what some viewed as radical counterculture behavior. Some argue that epistles such as Colossians were either written after Paul's death by someone close to him or were was produced by a Pauline school.

There may have been more scriptural references, but Fiorenza argues that the opponents of female leadership were writing from a patriarchal view. They communicated only portions of the traditions and portrayed only significant women in the early church.[30]

The question then rises, where does female leadership derive its support? One answer lies with Jesus. To get an understanding about how Jesus felt about women, biblical feminists and others turn to Christology. It is here that Jesus becomes the central focus, example, and role model for relationships and the Christian life.

Jesus broke many of the rigid social rules regarding male and female relationships.[31] He spoke to women in public (John 4). He paid attention to their plights and predicaments (John 8). Although for the most part uneducated, he listened to women and even opened the door to intellectual opportunities (Luke 10:38–45).

Jesus crossed gender and racial lines to reveal his messiahship to a woman and commission her to ignite an evangelistic effort in Sychar (John 4). Jesus, a human relations revolutionary, gave to the women at the tomb the command to carry the resurrection message as well as his emissaries (Mark 16:6–7; Matt. 28:7, 10; John 21:11–18). Jesus treated women as humans, not objects to be pitied or oppressed. He promoted egalitarian relationship between men and women.

Lisa Sergio in *Jesus and Woman* argues that Jesus broke with tradition in his recognition of women's equality. Every time he broke new ground in ministry, a woman played a central role. Ten of these occasions involved women who were unique individuals and yet at the same time were typical women of their time. Five were only known by their conditions—a Samaritan, a widow, a giving woman, the adulteress, or the sick woman—while the other five were known by their names: Mary of Magdala; Mary and Martha; Claudia Procula, wife of Pontius Pilate; and Mary, the mother of Jesus.[32]

In either case, liberation feminists, often while seeking to remain biblical, find support for female leadership by testing their assertions against women's experience. The experiences of women become a resource by which Christian tradition can be critically reassessed.[33]

Jarena Lee, the first woman to be licensed to preach in the A.M.E. Church, states about her call to leadership that she was fully persuaded that God had called her to preach. Julia Foote, the first woman ordained in the A.M.E. Zion Church, who met opposition from neighbors and friends, was also firmly convinced that she was called to a preaching career. Each of their ministries was fruitful. "Wherefore by their fruits, ye shall know them" (Matt. 7:20).

Foote wrote of many experiences in her autobiography. Among them was the occasion where she preached before crowds as large as five thousand during Holiness tent meetings. She related at one point that women were asked to produce credentials. These credentials were not to be of human origin, but were to be of a divine nature. If a woman could work a miracle, it would prove that she had a right to preach the gospel. Foote wrote that if it were necessary for women to do that, then it ought to be necessary for the brethren to show her the same credentials.[34]

Weems contends that African American women are challenged to identify with available biblical resources written by and for those in power against the powerless. Marginalized readers, such as African American women, must do all they can to recover the voice of the oppressed from the biblical text, which necessitates relying upon their own experience of oppression as a resource.[35]

There are some liberation feminists who believe that the Bible is too narrow in speaking only to concrete situations. Other disciplines, such as science, psychology, history, and sociology, significantly portray women's condition in particular and the human condition in general.[36]

Regarding 1 Timothy 2:11–15, Cermet raises an eyebrow and wonders what Paul meant by women learning in silence and to keep silent. Did he mean that Priscilla should have kept her mouth closed rather than correct Apollos? Or that Mary Magdalene should have kept her mouth closed rather than tell the disciples who did not come to the tomb early about the resurrected Christ?

In the later part of the pericope, verse 13 ("For Adam was first formed, then Eve"), Carmody believes that a mythology of disobedience was added to the mythology of creation. Women were subordinated because of the order of creation and because they initiated sin. She argues that the logic is inconsistent: Adam is either the responsible person, endowed with all that is noble in human nature, or he is equal to Eve, who is endowed with all that is sinful and weak. One cannot claim the right to all authority and responsibility of leadership today and then push the weakness on someone else tomorrow. One cannot be the teacher today and follow the false footsteps of one's student tomorrow.[37]

Grant sees similarities between the women's movement of the nineteenth century and the contemporary women's movement, and between the abolitionist thrust of the late 1800s and the civil rights era of the 1960s and 1970s.[38] The civil rights movement had elements that appealed to women, such as the "togetherness of all people" and "partnership." Many women who began to participate gravitated toward women's rights efforts. This was due to the racism of the women's movement.

Grant asserts that the civil rights movement gave way to a more radical women's liberation movement. Even though these two movements were juxtaposed at two separate times in history, the problem with all the feminist theologies, writes Grant, is that they are White and racist. Chief among the sources for feminism is women's experience; but it is White, not Black, women's experience. The Black woman's experience is different.

Black feminism grew out of the Black woman's struggle with tridimensional prejudicial experiences of race, class, and sex. Patricia Hill Collins suggests that Black feminist thought embodies special knowledge, created by African American women as the theoretical interpretation of their own reality.[39]

Black feminist theology is the drive to expose the various forms of oppression in race, class, and gender. The necessity of making distinctions between the experiences of Black and White women, leads Grant to focus upon a womanist theology.

The term *woman* refers to being fully grown, as opposed to girlish and immature. The term *womanist* refers to the woman-experiences of African American women. Author Alice Walker asserts that womanism is our being responsible, in charge, courageous, and bodacious enough to demand the right to think independently of both White and African American men and White women. Womanist theology is the courage to think theologically, independently of White men and women and African American men.[40]

Grant believes that womanist theology must engage the issues of class distinction among African Americans so that it does not become another bourgeois theology. It must engage the issues of class distinction among African Americans so that it does not become another meaningless thought to the disproportionately high percentage of women who occupy the poor and working-class stratum.[41]

The Bible is central to womanist theology, as well as the understanding that Jesus identified with the lowly and the least. The Bible, and the understanding of it, are to be engaged in the context of the Black woman's experience.

The church has not reneged on the challenge to continue its historical leadership in the struggle against oppression of the African American community. The church has stood against racism; it has not stood against the oppression of African American women with the same fervor. The church has often viewed African American women as enemies of, rather than partners in, community and kingdom build- ing. Ministers have used the Bible to justify subordinate roles of women within the institution.[42]

James Cone states that some African American male ministers have no problem rejecting Paul's commands to slaves "to be obedient to their masters" as valid justification of Black slavery, but they close the door to women with their stance regarding Paul's comments about silence and teaching.[43]

A large percentage of African American women have experienced being relegated to the lower rungs on the social ladder not only by White society, but according to Grant, by the African American church and the Black nationalist movement as well.

The womanist theological perspective shows encouraging signs of inclusiveness. It does not deny the value and worth of African Ameri- can men. The perspective considers both race and gender as valid ex- periential ground for "doing" theology.

It would serve no purpose to ascribe to another gender exclusive thought in the faith community. The African American community cannot afford to be divided within its ranks along gender or class dis- tinctions. It must rise to the egalitarian call of Jesus the Christ in seiz- ing the opportunity to follow his nonconformist liberating lifestyle. The distinctions of race, gender, and class are swallowed up by an agape love and reemerge into a new humanity.

THEOLOGICAL CHALLENGES

The theological challenges facing African American clergywomen are many. One challenge is to formulate a constructive Christology that includes both women and the larger African American community.

Another challenge is to explore "what Christ means in a society in which class distinctions are increasing." A high percentage of African American women are working-class, poor, single mothers, and heads of households. These women are being subjugated within the African American community.

If womanist theology is unable to meet this challenge of classism, then it will be viewed, indicates Grant, as another bourgeois theology, concerning itself only with issues pertinent to the middle class and excluding the majority of African American women.[44]

The next challenge is to explore the oppression of women and theological symbolism.[45] Feminism has challenged patriarchal hermeneutics, language, and symbolism. African American scholars must do the same, not only for African American women, but for the whole African American community as well.

The last challenge I will mention here is to make relevant application of theological perspectives for African American women and the African American community at large. The academy and the congregation must come together in dialogue to formulate, prepare, and express our common struggles, which broaden our expression of our knowledge of God.

Chapter five

BIBLICAL IMAGES OF FEMALE LEADERSHIP

"... and your sons and daughters shall prophesy ..." (Joel 2:28)

THE BIBLE HAS been used, or misused, to legitimize prejudicial distinctions of race, class, and religion as well as gender. Frank Chikane in *No Life of My Own* writes that he struggles with the reality that the Bible was used to brainwash the people and take their land in South Africa. The Bible was misused and the Christian faith misinterpreted. He had a choice to either reject the Bible or reappropriate it, reinterpret it, and put it in its rightful place.[1]

Dr. Cain Felder postulates that one of the challenges facing us today is to search for more adequate modes of hermeneutics to demonstrate that the Bible is relevant to Blacks and other Third World people, who are locked into the socioreligious framework of the Greco-Roman world.[2] Felder notes that the urgent agenda for biblical scholars and laity is a renewed commitment to acknowledgment of the integrity of all racial groups. Dr. Renita J. Weems views biblical interpretation and perspectives as challenging for African American women seeking a resource for shaping modern lifestyles. In many ways, the Bible has been antagonistic to modern female identity.[3]

Weems states that the challenge for scholars committed to a liberation perspective is to seek ways to explain the phenomenon of how persons from marginalized communities continue to view the Bible as a rich resource. She notes that it is a challenge because, in many ways, biblical authors do not view reality in the same way as marginalized communities do, and the Bible itself has been used to marginalized them.[4]

Feminist biblical interpreters use similar language when viewing female images in the Bible. They also use such words as *marginality, ancillary roles, liberation hermeneutics,* and *sex-role stereotyping,* rather than *racial stereotyping.*[5]

Alice Laffey notes that those who hold the Bible as the fount of faith and inspiration must understand the patriarchal prejudices of its authors and later interpreters.[6] She believes that biblical text, historically conditioned and produced by a patriarchal society, are to be viewed with suspicion. As women recognize that they have been objects of discrimination and injustice in the church and society, they must discover their history and create a new future.[7]

African American scholars must challenge the Eurocentric mindset for the sake of healthy scholarship and the African American community, notes Felder. It needs to be challenged in the same way that feminism challenged patriarchy and androcentrism.[8]

With this in mind, this chapter seeks to view female leaders whose presence survives in the Bible. The first part will briefly highlight female leaders in the Old Testament. The second will review female leaders in the New Testament. The next chapter will discuss the leadership behaviors of these biblical role models.

FEMALE LEADERSHIP IN THE OLD TESTAMENT

"Now Deborah, the wife of Lappidoth, was a prophet, and she was serving as a judge for the Israelites at that time." (Judg. 4:4)

For the most part, women in the Old Testament were identified by their relationship to their husbands, sons, or fathers. They were considered possessions of men. For example, rape was viewed not as violence done to the woman but to the man to whom she belonged, her father or her husband (Judg. 19–20).

Several women who functioned within their role of wife, mother, and homemaker emerged as leaders. Their leadership was not authority granted by an outside agency or the order of society but authority seized because of circumstances.

Naomi in the book of Ruth is an example. As the female head of her household, she led her family back home. She was the architect of

Ruth and Boaz's relationship. The couple later became progenitors of King David, figuring significantly into God's salvation plan of the coming Messiah.

Another example are the women at the tomb in Mark 16, Matt. 28, Luke 24, and John 20. We can recognize them as leaders because they mobilized people and resources toward a common goal and motivated others to help them. They provided a service, unselfishly doing the task without regard to the title or office. Jesus rewarded their presence by giving them the news of the resurrection to tell.

History often ironically records that in the final analysis, it is the quality of the deed and the character of the participants, whether male or female, and not their rank or title that really matters.[9]

Hebrew midwives Shiphrah and Puah in Exodus 1:18–22 were ordered by Pharaoh to kill all the male children that the Israelite women bore. The females were allowed to live, as they posed no threat to the hierarchy. The males of the minority posed a threat to the males of the majority, because manpower is a basic ingredient for any military action. Males of a minority also threaten the pure procreation of a majority.

Nancy Hastings, in her sermon "Let Pharaoh Go," in *And Blessed Is She,* writes that these two women played a large role in Israel's redemptive history by refusing to be apart of Pharaoh's secret and daring mission to kill all the boys.[10] Among their "saves" was a baby boy named Moses. This child's mother demonstrated great courage when she conspired to save her son from death (Exod. 2). Moses' mother planned and executed the deliverance into the enemy household. The child was raised in the sight of his birth mother by an unwed foster mother. And his mother was paid to nurse him (Exod. 2:9)!

Along with Miriam, Moses' sister, Pharaoh's daughter, each woman unknowingly kept him alive for the future mission of liberation. The women were not recognized religious leaders, yet they were used by God to further the salvation of a people.

Deborah, in Judges 4–5, had authority by title, office, and function. She is identified as a wife, judge, prophetess, and Mother of Israel. Deborah was a judge, a position granted to her by divine appointment. There is no biblical discussion about whether women were allowed to be judges or prophets. There is no biblical discussion about whether it was right for a wife to perform religious functions. There is no biblical discussion about whether other women were judges before her, or whether she had to prove her divine leadership before others would respect her position.

Deborah was a judge, not by common consent or human permission. She broke the patriarchal mold. She was a wife with (uncharacteristically) an outside job. She was a prophet with all the rights and privileges pertaining thereto. There is no biblical discussion of other prophets needing to validate the right to ascend to sit under the palm tree to judge all Israel. She did not have to defend her call. The apostle Paul was compelled to offer a defense of his appointment, but not Deborah.

Deborah, the judge and prophet, had a job and did it. She needed neither the permission of her husband nor the dispensation of humankind. Her performance was not predicated on human prerogatives. Only the fruitfulness of her ministry would validate or disavow her call. The burden of proof was not on Deborah but on God. God called Deborah, and it would be God's sovereign choice to empower her to speak, mediate, pontificate, and motivate God's people by the Creator's command.

Besides Deborah, Miriam, Huldah, the wife of Isaiah, and Noadiah also served in the prophetic ministry. Miriam was ranked equally with her brothers, Aaron and Moses (Num. 20:1). She was a psalmist who led the women in a songfest and impromptu dance-a-thon after crossing the Red Sea.

Little is known of the prophet Huldah except that she was a married woman, the wife of Shallum. She lived in Jerusalem, in "the college," where she was the keeper of the wardrobe (2 Kings 22:14). Ancient writing was discovered in the temple during renovations in reign of King Josiah. The king sent messengers to inquire of God about the validity of the writing. The messengers went to Huldah, not because she was a woman, but because she was a prophet. Obviously one whose word they trusted. Huldah foretold Jerusalem's ruin and Josiah's escape from trouble (2 Kings 22:15–22; 2 Chron. 34:22–25).

Both the Old and New Testaments use the words *prophetess* and *prophet*. The term *prophetess* is used to refer to women in the prophetic ministry in much the same way as *prophet* is used to refer to a man in the prophetic ministry.

The Old Testament also includes other women leaders, such as queens (the Queen of Sheba [1 Kings 10:1–10], Queen Athaliah [2 Kings 11:1–46], Esther [the book of Esther]) and queen mothers (Maachah [1 Kings 15:13]). There are also wise women (as in 2 Sam. 20:16) and witches, such as the one Saul sought in 1 Samuel 18:7–25. There are also false prophetesses in Israel, as shown in Ezekiel 13:17 and Revelation 2:20.

It seems that for far too many years, the only women continuously exhorted and instructed were those negative images used to oppress women. A steady diet of harlots, whores, prostitutes, foolish virgins, named and unnamed diseased and disruptive women have been paraded through pulpits and Sunday schools. Most notable are Eve, the waymaker for sin and shame, and Jezebel.

Jezebel, the wife of Ahab, king of Israel, is one of the most notable negative biblical queens. The daughter of Ethbaal, she came to the marriage comfortable with the loftiness of her upbringing. She brought her idol worship with her, and Ahab made for her a pagan shrine, angering God (1 Kings 16:31–34).

Enemies rarely got a second chance against Jezebel. Royal whims often became royal commands, such as when Naboth perished because he owned a piece of land near the palace. When Naboth refused to sell the property, the king could not take no for an answer. Jezebel would not take no for an answer, and she plotted his death (1 Kings 1:1–15).

Jezebel was a manipulator and controller, used to having her way. She thought she was above everyone: her husband, advisers , Jehovah's prophets, and God. But she was not above everyone. Her death sentence was pronounced and carried out by Jehu (1 Kings 21:23; 2 Kings 9:7,30–37).

FEMALE LEADERSHIP IN THE NEW TESTAMENT

"I commend unto you Phoebe our sister, which is a servant of the church which is at Cenchreae." (Rom. 16: 1)

The New Testament gives evidence of female leadership in several areas. In the prophetic role, are Anna, a prophetess (Luke 2:36) and the four daughters of Phillip (Acts 21:8–9).

Many women followed Jesus and witnessed his ministry. They included Mary, Mary Magdalene, Salome, Elizabeth, and others who heard his teachings and responded to his leadership. The woman at the well exhorted her neighbors (John 4). Mary Magdalene and Mary, the mother of James and Salome, came to the tomb early on resurrection morning (Mark 16:1; Matt. 28:1; John 20:1). The women carried the first message about the resurrected savior (Matt. 28:8; John 20:17–18).

Women functioned as fellow workers with Paul in the work of missions, evangelizing, and proclaiming the gospel. Paul mentions Euodia and Syntche (Phil. 4:2–3) and Prisca, another coworker who instructed Apollos in the correct doctrine of preaching (Acts 28:26).

One woman is called an "apostle" by Paul in Romans 16:7, as he referred to Andronicus and Junia. Some exegetes dispute this by saying that Junia is also a man's name. Several terms such as *diakonos, apostle,* and *coworker* were found in reference to men and women. They include Phoebe, *diakonos*; apostle, Junia; and coworker, Prisca.

Rosemary Ruether and Eleanor McLaughlin in *Women of Spirit* argue that Paul actually affirms female leadership in several ways. First, he uses the same Greek verb, *to labor* or *to toil,* in reference to his own work as well as that of the women. In Romans 16: 6–12, Paul commends Tryphena, Typhosa, Mary, and Persis, who "labored" hard.[11]

Paul admonishes the addressees of 1 Corinthians 16:16–18 to give recognition and be "subject to every coworker and laborer." In Philippians 4:2–3, he states explicitly that Euodia and Syntche "contend" with him by his side.

Ruether and McLaughlin considered Prisca to be one of Paul's prominent coworkers. With her husband, Aquila, she worked independently of Paul and not under Paul. The couple founded house churches in Ephesus, Corinth, and possibly Rome. When Paul greets them, he greets Prisca first.[12]

There is no indication that women were excluded from leadership or presiding in the house churches. Ruether and McLaughlin believe that the Deutero-Pauline literature known as the "household codes" and limited leadership of 1 Timothy 2 were a later patriarchal reaction to female leadership.[13]

In Philemon 2, Aaphia was a leader of a house church in Colossae along with Philemon and Arhippus. In Acts 16:14, it was Lydia's conversion that led to a church founded in Philippi, while Acts 12:12 speaks of a prayer meeting in the house of Mary, mother of John

Mark. Colossians 4:15 refers to the church in the house of Nympha.[14] In regard to Phoebe, Romans 16:1–7 refers to her as *diakonos* of the church at Cenchreae and "*Prostatis* of many and of myself as well." *Diakonos* means *servant, minister,* and *missionary. Prostatis* means *helper* and *patroness.*

Exegetes often translate *diakonos* as *deaconess* and *servant* in reference to women, and *deacon* when applied to male leaders. In Phoebe's case, it is often translated as *deaconess,* an auxiliary designation.

Phoebe's other title, *prostatis,* indicates a position of leadership. The person with this title was a leader, president, officer, or governor in the community. The word in 1 Thessalonians 5:2 refers to persons with authority in the community. In 1 Timothy 3:4–6 and 5:17, the word refers to the functions of elder, deacon, or bishop.[15] Therefore, Phoebe occupied a position of leadership in the church community of Cenchreae.

The letters of Paul have been used to deny women access to leadership roles; they have also been cited as proof that New Testament women were prominent leaders in the early church. Paul's letters reveal that women were coworkers with Paul. They were not limited to ministry among women only, and they participated in missionary functions. Women worked with Paul and independently of him.[16]

New Testament women were at the crux of birthing new churches. They opened their homes to prayer meetings and to house churches. These first-century women taught, prophesied, and led house churches with their husbands. Few title designations survive. They are often reinterpreted to marginal function and "honorable mentions."

Chapter six

LEADERSHIP STYLES AND BIBLICAL ROLE MODELS

THE HISTORICAL PERSPECTIVE and the biblical evidence of female prophetic leadership make several things very clear. First, women such as Huldah, Deborah, and Phoebe served as leaders in the religious community in spite of cultural taboos and social biases. They could not be denied, nor was their presence totally edited out. They were considered the "yes, but . . ." exception rather than the rule.

Second, female leaders were subjected to intense opposition within and outside of their respective religious bodies. Third, these female leaders suffered similar prejudices as other women in male-dominated fields such as business, sports, and medicine. However, in the church, the women labored and continue to do so under the use and misuse of theological perspectives and biblical interpretation, which in essence says that even God thinks you are a second-class citizen![1]

Not Without a Struggle could easily settle for cataloging female leaders in the biblical and historical perspectives. That is not enough. What is of interest is the reflection on female biblical leader images to see how these role models engaged in leadership. What were their leadership styles according to modern dictates? Were there any discernible leader behaviors, and do they contribute to a leader hermeneutic for female leaders today?

In order make such a study, we must first discuss what leadership is and its importance to the church in general and African American congregations in particular.

LEADERSHIP

Leadership is an important component of strong and competent ministry. From the African American perspective, leadership is not only necessary but demanded. According to Floyd Massey and Samuel McKinney, in *Church Administration in the Black Perspective*, even if a pastor wanted to lag behind, he or she would be pushed, forced to the head of the army, or crushed in the criticism.[2]

The leader of a congregation in the African American tradition must be equipped with administrative tools of leadership to enable the flock to function efficiently and effectively on a variety of levels, within and without its walls. The pastoral leader is challenged with a multiplicity of problems, often with limited resources.[3]

All leaders, especially in the African American perspective, must also be advocates of truth, justice, and equal rights on behalf of the constituents globally. Leaders must also be involved in the immediate environment.

Ministers in the African American context are shaped by their own experiences with racism, sexism, oppression, and economic deprivation. And, in turn, must be leaders to people who have historically been victimized by institutional oppression and persistent racism. Leaders in the African American church may even be called upon to act not only in spiritual matters but political, social, economic, and urban roles as well.

There is a continuous need for prophetic leadership to rise up against those who would nullify the work of Jesus and question his mission in this world. The criteria for inclusion are still the same (Col. 3:1–11; Gal. 3:28). The universal sovereignty of Jesus Christ is the center of a new humanity. All shallow distinctions such as race, class, sex, and cultural and social background are confronted by a tidal wave of communal love. They find no validity in the body of Christ. The criteria are based on being buried with Christ in baptism and raised up to be a part of the universal community.

Cornel West in *Prophetic Fragments* notes that Christian rhetoric and moral argument are not effective strategies against torture and other dehumanizing forces such as slavery, racism, and sexism. This kind of conversation will not have a major impact on those who perpetuate such evil.[4]

If we desire to see torture cease (and other divisive human activities), we will be able to achieve this by applying institutional pressure and social force. West feels that the social force needed is to be found within the prophetic wing of Christian churches.

The leader must lead the church to measure the world always in the light of ideal Christian love and relate this ideal to prevailing systems of power and control. The ideal must then commit itself to the struggle for dignity against systems that deny it.[5]

The conditions of the African American community, asserts James H. Harris, demand strong ministerial leadership. The leader and the congregation are both necessary in developing critical responses to issues of freedom and justice. The gospel still must be preached, but the minister-leader must be involved in the liberation of African Americans from the oppression prevalent in the country.[6]

Effective leadership, then is important for strong and competent ministry. This is especially critical in the African American perspective, as we need leaders who can create, articulate, and communicate a liberating vision paradigm; enable others to be more than they have been; provide prophetic insight; and urgently help those they influence to recognize that there is a hope and a future.

WHAT IS LEADERSHIP?

Leadership is a word with several different meanings. It is used to refer to those who occupy the role of a leader as well as to the special traits of those leaders. *Leadership* is often used to describe a set of functional responsibilities that must be utilized to maintain an organization's task.[7]

Leadership, simply stated, is the ability to bring people together for the accomplishment of common goals.[8] It is the process that blends the achieving of those goals with the maintenance of the organization, the process of keeping the group or organization together and/or expanding.[9]

Often there are multiple expectations and tensions between what is unreal and what is ideal in terms of the numerous functional expectations of the performance of the clergy role. Campbell and Reierson, in *The Gift of Administration,*[10] tend to agree that the minister is expected to be preacher, liturgist, counselor, friend, teacher, social-change agent, public-spirited citizen, responsible parent, loving spouse, accountant, bookkeeper, visionary, secretary, planner, organizer, and perhaps we should add butcher, baker, and candlestick maker.

The Bible has a lot to say about the multiplicity of roles and functions. Jesus used two words to describe those who followed him: one is *disciple,* or learner; the other is *apostle,* or one sent or commissioned to represent another.

The minister is expected to have faith in Christ, first. When Jesus chose those to follow him, he first called them into a relationship with him (John 1:15). He then asked them to sacrifice their usual occupations and to follow him.

A minister is expected to proclaim the gospel. The minister is like the town crier or a herald in the marketplace. He or she is the announcer in and outside of the church.

The minister is a steward. As "stewards of the mysteries of God" (1 Cor. 4:1), it is the role of ministers to provide the family of God or household of faith with the things that nourish, strengthen, and edify the body of Christ.

Through the Word of God, it can also be seen that the minister is a servant (Mark 10:42–43), a collaborator and coworker with Christ. In 1 Thessalonians 3:2, Paul indicates that he has sent Timothy, his brother and God's coworker, in the gospel of Christ.

It is through the minister, the agent, the vessel, instrument and coworker that Christ heals, saves, and works. That is not to say that it is only through the minister that God works.

The Bible is filled with many rich images for the pastor and minister. There are priests, prophets, prophetesses, sages, elders, pastors, bishops, deacons, and missionaries. Yet there is one role that has not been mentioned, and that is a leader.

Robert D. Dale, in *Pastoral Leadership*, notes that pastors must be leaders and provide leadership in their respective churches.[11] In the urban setting, the pastor becomes a leader in denominational affairs, politics, community service, education, and business.[12] Dale also describes leadership as an action-oriented, interpersonal influencing process. It involves visions, initiative, communication, shared objectives, and the transformation of followers into new leaders.[13]

In *Ministers as Leaders,* Dale quotes James MacGregor as stating that there are two types of leaders: transacting and transforming. The transacting leader is one who exchanges one thing for another, bargains in order to trade values, gives something to receive something, allocates existing resources and manages them. The transforming leader engages followers by satisfying higher motivations and needs. The result is a mutually stimulating relationship that converts followers into leaders. The transforming leader inspires, mobilizes, exalts, uplifts, evangelizes, and raises the level of human conduct. Dale describes the transacting leader as a custodian and the transformer as a builder-motivator.

To Dale, a leader is one who "sizes up" the situation and chooses a course of action suited for that situation. A leader needs to size up his or her pastoral settings on a regular basis, choosing and changing tactics as needed.

A leader seeks and follows the guidance of the Holy Spirit. The leader is one who plans the program in cooperation with the Holy Spirit, allowing the situation to determine the tactics. Such was the case of Nehemiah, who prayed to God for four months before returning to Jerusalem (Neh. 2–6). He gained a consensus of the people and then planned a strategy of rebuilding Jerusalem's wall, changing his tactics as his enemies changed theirs. Thus, a leader also secures the cooperation of officers and lay members, enlists new member leaders, promotes teamwork, and inspires loyalty.

Leaders can have a profound effect on those who follow them. Leaders create new ideas, fresh outlooks, and new movements and institutions. Leaders can leave an imprint on a church, a community and a nation, such as the imprint left by such leaders as Nannie Helen Burroughs and Martin Luther King Jr.

Dale describes leaders as wavemakers. Leaders make waves that continuously lap upon the shores of our institutions. Because these waves can be destructive tidal waves and/or ripples, Dale feels that *how* a leader does something is just as important as *what* the leader does.

Arthur Adas, in *Effective Leadership for Today's Church*, describes leadership style as focusing in on the way a leader functions. The leader's style is characterized by the strategies used in working with other people.

Leadership style has also been termed "leader behavior."[14] It is also the manner of expressing a leader's values and executing the work. *Style* refers to the distinctive approach that a leader has to ministry and to other persons.

Andrew Watterson in *Pastoral Leadership* describes a pastoral leader by referring to Exodus 18, on the occasion of Jethro's advice to son-in-law, Moses, about his leadership. Moses was sitting to judge the people from morning to evening. Jethro observed that to continue to do so would "surely wear away, both thou, and this people that is with thee; thou art not able to perform it thyself alone" (Exod. 18:18).

Moses was a leader with management problems. He had constant morale problems, which erupted in murmurings and complaints. Moses had food and water problems that laid a foundation for mutiny. It was the handling of a particular personnel problem that cost him a trip into the Promised Land. Moses was a great leader and paradigm buster. His managerial capabilities were a thorn in his flesh.

Jethro's wise counsel was not a substitute for his prophetic gifts or divine call. It increased his effectiveness and efficiency as a leader.

The same God who calls a man or woman to the gospel ministry will also equip him or her to serve. The Creator equips men and women through educational preparation, biblical and theological training, on-the-job training, and other life and ministerial experiences.

LEADERSHIP AND AFRICAN AMERICAN CLERGYWOMEN

The vast majority of published literature on leadership issues does not discuss African American clergywomen breaking into all-male church leadership ranks. Many women have had to read between the lines to find the leadership strategies and information to fit their needs and experience.

Not Without a Struggle is contextualization. Contextualization recognizes the impact of struggles and experiences of African American clergywomen as they develop leadership competencies.

Many African American clergywomen face similar pressures and challenges. These experiences include the constant pressure to explain and defend the call to the gospel ministry; the pressure that your success or failure affects the women who follow you; and the realization that you must be better than, or just as good as, the best male for the position in order to be considered.

The number of African American clergywomen is increasing. But there is still a lack of role models. Goals are easier to set and pursue when we can visualize others who mirror or demonstrate the same or similar goals. There is also a scarcity of mentors, male and female. Mentor relationships provide advice, information, and someone who can help move you into positions of greater responsibilities.

African American clergywomen often serve in isolation. With one or only a few other women in the ministry in the same locale, there is also a need for female network or support groups to share information and exchange ideas. Several clergywomen shared during the Women Surviving in Ministry seminar that they resented being pitted against each other for the *one* position designated as the "woman's spot." They felt they had to compete with each other not in areas of skill, ability, or intellect, but in a kind of "beauty contest" or "popularity contest" for a token appointment. At times they struggled to get pulpit assignments no one wanted, not even their male counterparts. One clergywoman felt that women are often assigned a particularly challenging pulpit either to "test their mettle" or to discourage them from serving altogether.

These pressures and challenges are also felt by African American men in White-dominated circumstances and by young males breaking into new leadership positions. The same pressures and challenges faced by some African American clergywomen were also faced by women in male-dominated society.

Dr. Beth Milwid writes in *Working with Men* that many of the 125 women she interviewed were uncomfortable with the tremendous pressure to achieve.[15] The women acknowledged that the professional's first task, male or female, is to prove his or her ability and to try to fit in. The difference is that men are expected to succeed while women are expected to fail.

The minority women she interviewed indicated that the pressure to prove themselves at work with males was similar to African Americans having to prove themselves in White society. The survival skills they developed as the sole or one of few African Americans working in White society prepared them to be the sole or one of few females in male-dominated organizations and vocations.[16]

Many women were in the unenviable position of learning at new jobs at the same time learning how to survive in a male culture. They came with many assumptions. Two core assumptions of many women, notes Dr. Milwid, are that hard work and achievement will be rewarded and that men will be friends with them just as they were in school.[17]

Men, notes Dr. Milwid, also have generalizations and assumptions about the women they work with. One of the assumptions is that women are by nature "too nice," "too emotional," or "too unstable" for professional business life. Another assumption involves a set of stereotypes that casts women into the role of daughter, sister, or mother by male colleagues. Men with few experiences working with female professionals rely on family relationships as the framework for coping.

In the first few months as the pastor of one of the three churches I have been privileged to serve as pastor, many men "adopted" me as the daughter or granddaughter who needed their protection and admiration. Women also "adopted" me as the daughter or granddaughter they never had or always wanted. It was only through consistent and insistent hard work as a professional minister and not the role of "daddy's girl" that helped them begin to see me as their chief undershepherd of the church. They woke up one day and realized I was their pastor!

Dr. Milwid notes that by willpower and time, women usually pass their tests on the job. But the intent to disprove generalizations often takes its toll physically. Women become victims of perfectionism, the superwoman syndrome, and other stress-related problems.

MALE AND FEMALE LEADERSHIP

There is a difference between the manner in which men and women engage in leadership behavior. Authors such as Patricia Aburdene and John Naisbitt in *Megatrends for Women*, Sally Helgesen in *The Female Advantage: Women's Ways of Leadership*, and Judy B. Rosener, professor in the Graduate School of Management at the University of California–Irvine, writing in the *Harvard Business Review*, tend to agree.[18]

Male leadership models and definitions generally can be traced to sports, the military, and metaphors developed during the industrial era. However, the country has moved from an industrial to an information age. The country has also joined the world economy, and the environment is rapidly changing. The "drill sergeant" leader and the pyramid structures of management are not working as well as they used to.

The newer models of leadership include characteristics usually attributed to women's value systems or behaviors. These include shared power, encouraged participation, and information sharing and communication.

Earlier male models relied on characteristics generally attributed to men. These characteristics included giving orders, issuing demands, rewards for performance, and punishment for inadequate performance. Aburdene and Naisbitt describe male leaders as "transactional" and women leaders as "transforming." Male leaders, generally speaking, rely on order and rank; demand respect; limit and define, impose discipline;

are rigid, command and control; have little time for people; reach up and down; evaluate performance; know all the answers; believe in rank and function hierarchically.

Women's leadership objective is change, not control. Women leaders, generally speaking, act as role models; value creativity; facilitate; teach archetypes; establish mutual contracts for specific results; reach out; are growth-oriented, visionary, master motivators; have infinite time for people; are flexible, holistic, and personal.

While men operate hierarchically, women network. Men rely on rank, women on connections. Men present the image that they know all the answers. Women tend to ask the right questions. While all men do not fit the above descriptions, neither do all women.

It is interesting to note that Aburdene and Naisbitt describe women as "transforming" leaders. This is the same term used by author Leighton Ford in *Transforming Leadership*. Ford indicates that "transforming" leadership is Jesus' way of creating vision, shaping values, and empowering change. It is this Jesus leadership model that should guide both men and women.

CHARACTERISTICS OF FEMALE LEADERSHIP

When women began entering male arenas such as business and religion, there were few mentors to guide them. They had few or no resources from sports or the military from which to draw. They were forced to find their own way.

In the beginning, many authors such as Betty L. Harragan in *Games Mother Never Taught You* advised women to learn male leadership models. and to imitate male leadership strategies. But these strategies were not working well for anyone, male or female.

Women began to develop their own strategies based on expressing their female strengths rather than denying gender traits. The characteristics of these female leaders are rooted in their experiences in female social roles. The traditional role of caring for others then become the basis of the leadership skills of supporting, caring, and bringing out the best in congregants or employees.

Women leaders, generally speaking, encourage participation, share power and information, enhance other people's self-worth, and get others excited about their work. Women leaders tend to solicit input, teach, and create positive working environments.

Empowering is a major component of female leadership. Women tend to empower others to feel confident to act on their own authority. The person empowered feels that the leader respects his or her judgment. If a person makes a mistake, many leaders who happen to be women use that as an opportunity to teach rather than to humiliate or berate a colleague.

Empowerment is one major component of women's leadership, and creating the environment for it to operate in is another. Women leaders tend to discard the hierarchy or pyramid structure for what is called by some the "web." The leader is at the center, rather than at the top, where she believes it is lonely. At the center, the leader is able to construct a series of concentric circles and then to connect the circles at any point without being boxed in or limited in structure.

AFRICAN AMERICAN FEMALE LEADERSHIP AND EUROCENTRIC (WHITE) FEMALE LEADERSHIP

As women's experience is a valid starting point for "doing" theology, women's experience is also a valid starting point for "doing" characteristics of women's leadership. The African American clergywoman does not draw upon the same sources that define and are by nature rooted in Eurocentric experiences.

As mentioned previously, the female characteristics of leadership are rooted in women's experience in traditional social roles. The African American woman's characteristics of leadership are also rooted in historical and present social roles.

The female leadership strength of supporting and encouraging arises from the traditional role of taking care of others. African American women have these experiences as well. However, it is important to note that many, who were enslaved or who served in menial servant positions, not only took care of others in their own homes but in their masters' or employers' homes as well. African American women are products of their struggle with racism, sexism, and classism. Their style of leadership is a legacy from the Mothers of Struggle, who raised other peoples' babies while their own were sold away; who dreamed great dreams while doing menial labor; who learned how to collect the pieces that life gave them and quilt them together as a covering for the whole family; who marched, sat in, picketed, protested, and were jailed.

From these experiences African American women developed their leadership characteristics. This possibly explains why relatively few African American women adhere to exclusionary philosophies such as feminism; rather they lean towards womanism, an inclusionist perspective that includes racial and gender concerns.

The African American woman leader, generally speaking, is an in-charge leader, courageous, bold enough to demand, independent of both Eurocentric men and women and African American men. She often focuses on people, because systems and structures generally deny her access. She keeps her eye on future horizons, because she knows the best is yet to come. She is an innovator who challenges the status quo. Often she has managed to function as both the only woman and the only African American leader, clergy or otherwise, in many organizations.

African American women leaders tend to bring a care and concern for the African American community to whatever positions they hold. Some, not all, look for ways to incorporate a social justice perspective to their job or congregation. Unlike her Eurocentric counterpart, she is sensitive to exclusionary policies and tactics that are racist more than sexist.

In summary, there are distinct differences between African American female leadership characteristics and Eurocentric (White) female leadership. The tasks remain similar. They include those activities that bring people together for the achievement of common goals: making decisions, setting and achieving goals, and maintaining or expanding the organization.

The techniques of leadership, or the systematic methodological approach by which these tasks of leadership are achieved, may be similar. The style, or the combination of distinct behaviors that determine the manner in which these tasks are achieved, however, is different. The crucible in which these styles and techniques are developed, is different. Leader styles and behaviors were developed in the cane brakes, cotton fields, and sweatshops; they were developed in other people's kitchens, while taking care of other people's children and living life as a minority within a minority, separate and not equal.

Therefore, the attitude surrounding the characteristics of women's leadership is different. This attitude impacts on loyalty. Many African American women leaders are less likely to join Eurocentric women leaders to oust an African American man because he is male. To the African American female leader, he is an African American first, then a man. African American women leaders may be flexible in some areas, like their Eurocentric counterparts. But many African American women leaders are rigid when racial issues are raised.

BIBLICAL ROLE MODELS

One method of examining biblical role models is to use a theoretical leadership model. The model that will be used here is one developed by Dr. Robert D. Dale in *Pastoral Leadership.* He is professor of pastoral leadership and church ministry at Southeastern Baptist Theological Seminary in Wake Forest, North Carolina.

Leaders can use this model to identify their style, or the characteristic manner in which they express their values in approaching their work. The style of a leader can also be characterized as "leader behavior," or the distinctive approach that a leader has to ministry and to others.

Other authors, such as Charles J. Keating in *The Leadership Book* and Bennie Goodwin in *The Effective Leader,* also give basic leadership style distinctions.

Goodwin uses three basic leadership styles, the "I" leader, the "they" leader, and the "we" leader:

1. "I" leaders center the group's activities around themselves and their desires.
2. "They" leaders function by not leading the group continuously. They research the problem, summarize findings, make recommendations, and move on. "They" leaders function as consultants.
3. "We" leaders are active members of the group, seeking to unite the group, engage in team building, and along with the group to identify goals.

Instead of three, Keating uses four basic styles, with each addressing some portion of the relationship and task functions:

1. The "country club" style devotes a lot of attention to relationship, relaxation, and camaraderie. Work is often sporadic.
2. The "high-task and low-relationship" style is very directive. It works well in situations that are losing or have lost their sense of direction.
3. The "high-task and high-relationship" style calls for clarity of purpose as well as the nurturing of interpersonal relationships in the group.
4. The "low-task and low-relationship" style works well with mature groups, where the purpose is clearly defined.

Dale, for descriptive purposes, utilizes a similar range of four style possibilities. His styles fall also into two main groups, task and relationship functions or people and production. Dale terms his four basic styles catalyst, commander, encourager, and hermit. He believes that no one is likely to use any style in its pure form but rather will use various aspects of one or two.[19]

We usually have one preferred or dominant style, with another serving as backup. We switch to the second style automatically, in much the same way that we automatically switch to certain behaviors during an emergency. For many, the back-up style is unlike the dominant one. When everything is going well, a leader will behave in one way. But suddenly, someone goes for the jugular, and the style that emerges can be the reverse or opposite; it is almost a Jekyll-and-Hyde change.

Dale's model of leadership style is adapted to a local church and pastoral perspective. His terminology helps church leaders to visualize more clearly the available style options.

The Catalyst. A catalyst creates a positive organizational atmosphere, where positive goals are reached and people are built up actively.[20] The catalyst is a balanced leader, integrating missions and morale, goals and personal needs. This type of leader takes the initiative in relationships, demonstrating friendliness, approachability, and vigor. Dale further describes the catalyst as active, positive, and flexible. This leader is a patient planner and persistent implementer, who sticks by the task and the people. Catalysts train, organize, and delegate to achieve the goals of the organization. Thus they need a cadre of trained persons to execute the plans of the congregation.[21]

The Encourager. Dale characterizes the encourager as employing an empathetic style. This leader is concerned more about relations than organizational goals and about morale more than mission.[22] This leadership style is people-centered. Encouragers listen well, nurture others, and work well in settings where there is membership stress and conflict, notes Dale. They are nondirective in work approach, leaving organizational and relational agendas in the hands of others. This style promotes "passive-optimism" and permissiveness.[23]

The Hermit. The hermit-style leader is one who is uncomfortable with organizational goals and relationships. These leaders are withdrawn and/or shy, often actually following their followers. Dale states that they may be withdrawn naturally or made so by congregational abuse. Hermit leaders are reticent to confront people or goals when differences arise. Their style is to hide or postpone action. A leader who uses this style on a daily basis becomes vulnerable, and the organization becomes stagnant.[24]

The Commander. Dale characterizes the commander style as the most efficient. The commander communicates directives clearly and expects followers to follow immediately. These leaders are active "people-approachers," who can be autocratic and rigid in putting goals ahead of people.[25] Commanders impose their own goals on the organization and often take aggressive action even when the situation does not demand it.

The commander style is the type of behavior that takes over situations fraught with anxiety. This is a basic principal of rehabilitative medicine. The commander-style leader works well in emergencies and short-range situations. Immediate reactions and results occur when these leaders are in charge. The leader's behavior creates pressure and conflict in the organizations they serve. Their aggressive style keeps expectations high, a "we-versus-they" atmosphere and a directive life and leadership attitude.[26]

It is possible to apply the basic four descriptions of this model to female biblical leaders. The dominant leadership style of Ruth would be the encourager style. Hagar qualifies for the hermit style. Hebrew midwives Shiprah and Puah were commanders, keeping newborn male Hebrew children alive against the orders of Pharaoh (Exod. 1–2). We will further examine the four basic leadership styles of Dale's model by applying them to female biblical role models Esther, Deborah, and the Queen of Sheba.

Deborah was chosen because no other female prophets are reported as serving at the same time. She was a minority. As such, she served alone without benefit of other female role models in a patriarchal social climate. Deborah was also a wife, with a management position outside the home. She was a dual-career woman.

Esther was chosen also because she was a minority, Jewish within a Persian majority. She demonstrated leadership within the patriarchal system of her time, as queen consort. Many African American clergywomen must exercise their leadership within the limitations established by church judicatories and tradition.

The Queen of Sheba was chosen because of her African ancestry. She was not a queen consort but a ruler with her own authoritative power. This queen moved with confidence and political astuteness to accomplish her task when visiting King Solomon. Many African American clergywomen demonstrate the similar leadership qualities.

It is not always easy to discern the dominant leadership style of biblical leaders. Some are more obvious than others. Although the four female leaders examined display characteristics of the style attributed to them, they may reflect other styles as well.

DEBORAH: THE COMMANDER

Judges, such as Deborah (Judg. 4–5), played an important role during the time when Israel's form of government was a loose confederation of twelve tribes. This was the time following Joshua and just prior to rise of the prophet Samuel. The Israelites were in a constant state of spiritual flux. They were turning to and away from God in a cycle of sin, judgment, and oppression. The judges could also serve as military leaders who rescued the people from their physical enemies. They also were God's instruments of restoration and reconciliation.

Deborah is identified as a wife, judge, prophet, and Mother of Israel. She performed the functions of her office at a time when the social climate was perhaps nonsupportive of a woman in a role other than those described earlier.

One Jewish morning prayer reflected great patriarchal sentiments; in it men blessed God for not having been created female.[27] Women who functioned in roles out of step with patriarchal society were considered exceptions. These exceptions were accepted and valued as long as they remained just that—exceptions. Whenever it looked like the exception might become the rule, men rebelled.[28]

There is evidence in both the Old and New Testament that God, unlike societies and church institutions, gives women the authority of office. The same is true for other marginalized groups.

Israel came under the cruel oppression of Jabin, a Canaanite king and the mighty captain of his army, Sisera, after the death of Ehud. The Israelites cried to God for help (Judg. 4:1–3). Deborah, who held court under a palm tree, sent for Berak, a military chief. She confronted him with God's command to take an army of ten thousand and defeat Sisera. Berak complied when Deborah agreed to go with him into battle. She joined him in leading the military offensive that brought about the victory that God promised. Following the victory, Deborah judged Israel peacefully for forty years.

Deborah's dominant leadership style is a commander style. This style works well in a crisis, when an immediate response is needed. The short-term goal of liberation overshadowed any other goals such as unification of the tribes. Deborah articulated her directives, clearly pressing for immediate action. She established the goal of victory over Sisera and then set out to put in place the necessary personnel to carry out the job.

The commander-style leader is active in relationships. Deborah did not wait for Berak to come to her. She sent for him. She was willing to do whatever was necessary to get the job done, even go into battle.

The commander-style leader tends to be sure of her position, her proper course of action, and her follower's positions. Deborah falls into this category. There is no indication that she was concerned about whether others approved or disapproved of her behavior. There is no indication of concern over whether other women had previously served as judges. There is no indication that she consulted with other committees or groups before deciding on a course of action. Deborah was a commander in that situation. She saw the problem, indicated the necessary course of action, and then proceeded to participate in the outcome.

ESTHER: THE CATALYST

Esther, a cousin of Mordecai, was chosen by King Ahasuerus as his wife after he deposed Queen Vashti. King Ahasuerua ruled 127 provinces around 475 B.C.E. from India to Ethiopia. Esther lived in opulence, reclining with guests and other royal family members on couches of gold and silver, drinking out of golden goblets of which no two were alike.[29] Mordecai told Esther to keep her Jewish heritage secret from the king. He also revealed a plot to kill her new husband.

Haman, an ambitious Amelekite and a favorite of the king, conceived a plot to slaughter the Jews by using the king's edict to guarantee the outcome. Mordecai asked Esther to intercede with the king on behalf of her people. After an initial hesitation, she complied.

Characteristically as a catalyst-style leader, Esther patiently plotted and planned her course of action. She planned her entrance into the king's court and courted his favor through two banquets. Even as queen, Esther could not go into the presence of the king without an invitation. To do so would mean certain death. But Esther, having planned and prepared, demonstrated persistence by sticking to her task and standing with her people, although it endangered her life.

She involved others in the achievement of her goals, integrating both morale and mission. Esther involved the members of her personal household staff by entreating them to pray and fast with her. She may not have told the king of her heritage, but it appears she still practiced the spiritual disciplines of prayer and fasting.

The catalyst leader is flexible. She is able to handle a variety of personalities. Esther invited both her enemy and her husband to her banquets. At the first banquet, the king remembered Mordecai, who revealed the plot to kill him. Haman, who hated Mordecai, now honored him publicly. At the second banquet, Esther revealed Haman's plot to slaughter the Jews and hang Mordecai. The king issued a second edict so that the Jews could defend themselves. The occasion is still remembered today during the Jewish feast of Purim.

Esther demonstrated the steady positive forward motion of the catalyst-style leader. These leaders know what they want and what they stand for.

THE QUEEN OF SHEBA: THE CATALYST

The Queen of Sheba, whose leadership example is mentioned in the discussion of female leadership examples from ancient Africa in chapter 2, is also a catalyst-style leader. She is described in the Old Testament, in 1 Kings 10 and 2 Chronicles 9, as having visited King Solomon.

The name of the Queen of Sheba is not mentioned in the biblical account. Other sources, such as Josephus, refer to her as the Queen of Egypt and Ethiopia. Larry Williams and Dr. Charles S. Finch indicate that in southern Arabia she was called Belkis, and in other documents she is called Makeda.[30]

Queen Makeda ascended the throne following the death of her father to rule the large Ethiopian empire for fifty years. The empire is theorized as including parts of Upper Egypt, Ethiopia, parts of Arabia, Syria, Armenia, and India. Williams and French cite other sources that indicate that she ruled with justice, fortitude, and wisdom.[31]

In order to rule her empire, it was necessary for Makeda to engage in extensive trade to ensure its economic survival. Her astuteness as a commercial trader is observed by the boldness of her trade relations in the markets of Damascus and Gaza. The trade network she organized was by the sea and was effectively manned by vigilant Ethiopian merchants. The leader of these merchants was Tamrin, who is described in the *Kebra Nagast* as a wise man.

The biblical account of the queen's visit to Solomon reveals a few things about her that would indicate a dominant leadership style. The Bible notes that the queen came on a visit to test Solomon with hard questions. She came with a caravan that included camels laden with gold, precious stones, and spices. The length of the journey and the impressive wealth indicate extensive planning on her part. Catalyst-style leaders plan and meticulously carry out their plans. These leaders needs other trained people around them to execute their plans. The queen certainly must have traveled with advisors, staff, and maybe even military personnel.

The Queen of Sheba was an observant leader. The biblical account indicates that she observed the wisdom of Solomon, the details of his household, and even the clothing of his servants. She even watched closely the offerings he made to God in the temple. The queen was generous to Solomon, giving him 120 talents of gold and large quantities of spices and precious stones (1 Kings 10:10). Catalyst-style leaders not only move forward steadily upon their plans but model behavior to those around them. She gave gifts to Solomon first. He responded in kind and later granted her all her heart desired.

Williams and French indicate that this visit between two royals probably involved the making of actual commercial and trade agreements. The queen's questions pertained to commerce, and she was actually

feeling him out as a partner or an opponent. A military peace agree-
ment may have been what was granted to the Queen of Sheba.

Catalyst-style leaders are often open to initiating new relationships.
They are friendly and open in their approach. The Queen of Sheba
models this behavior in her journey to visit Solomon.

Dale's leadership style model applies aptly to these biblical female
leaders. Their experiences model qualities and behaviors that African
American clergywomen can distinguish. Each of these biblical role
models also has similar distinguishing characteristics. Each was a leader
who challenged the existing social paradigm. Each challenged the status quo, whether she was a prophet or queen consort. Deborah, Esther,
and the Queen of Sheba were pioneers breaking new ground. They
took risks that endangered their safety or their lives.

Each of these role models also encouraged or enabled others to
follow their lead or to do it with them. They were enablers and
empowerers—Deborah and Esther more than the Queen of Sheba.
Deborah and Esther shared a hope for the future. Jesus would later lift
up the Queen of Sheba as an example to be emulated (Matt. 12:42).

Chapter seven

A PROFILE OF AFRICAN AMERICAN WOMEN IN THE MINISTRY AND WOMANIST LEADER-STYLE RESPONSES

WHO IS THE African American clergywoman? How does she respond to leadership rejection? Who does she listen to? Who does she call upon in a crisis? And what about mentors, role models, education, friends, and the balancing act of personal and ministerial life?

There are few resources that open a window allowing others, including other clergywomen, to peak into the hearts and minds of African American women in ministry. The pressure to prove their competence in a "racexist" society (the double-barreled shotgun paradigm of racism and sexism) enhances isolationism. Clergywomen often learn to keep some things to themselves and ponder them in their hearts (Luke 2:19).

Like women in business, they try not to show publicly that things are rough. They are intent on disproving the "hysterical woman" stereotype, especially in their initial years in the male-dominated field. In spite of anxiety and exhaustion in the struggle, they keep their feelings to themselves, determined not to show publicly what is really going on.[1]

Sixty-four African American women in ministry were surveyed, and one hundred African American clergywomen were interviewed about twenty-eight questions in a variety of areas, including education, leadership, church, personal life, and spiritual life.

Admittedly, the survey and interviews are limited by region and denomination. They do, however, represent a valuable collection of ideas, experiences, behaviors, and habits of contemporary African American clergywomen. Their responses can be used for further dialogue among clergywomen, students, men, and women colaboring in God's ministerial vineyard.

African American clergywomen are paradigm busters, making history and pioneering paths for generations to follow. Their shared experiences become a body of material for other "Daughters of Thunder" to reflect and fall back on.

BOOMERS AND BUSTERS

The membership of many churches in the United States seems to consist of men and women from the generation dominated by World War II and the separate-but-equal days of Eisenhower and King. The paradigms for their way of "doing church" were cut from cloth woven by predictable social roles.

Baby boomers represent perhaps the next-largest generational group in the church in many parts of the country. They are men and women born between 1946 and 1964. Their lives were shaped by the civil rights movement, the Vietnam War, the sexual revolution, urban riots, and the assassinations of King and the Kennedys.

The baby busters are those born after 1964, who are products of a rapidly changing world village and technological advancements. They are quite comfortable cruising the information superhighway. They prefer not to do without what boomers never had, namely beepers, cellular phones, fax machines, and situational ethics.

The parents of boomers move in a church world characterized by process. The process or step-by-step methodology of "doing church" frustrates both boomer and busters. The busters, especially, are frustrated by the methods of the process crowd, being a "right-now-to-day–don't walk, run–have-it-your-way" generation.

Parents of boomers were astonished over just receiving their information by means such as portable radios, cassettes, compact discs, and computers. Boomers and busters not only hear their information, they see it; they not only hear music, they see it in music videos; they not only read the newspaper every morning, they scan major newspapers all over the world on the Internet.

The majority of women interviewed and responding to the survey were boomers and busters. To them, "Depression" refers to either a bad mood that refuses to go away or a weather disturbance located over the Caribbean, but not to a catastrophic economic event that millions had to live through.

Their attitude toward ministry is like the Nike commercials that proclaim "Just do it!" They are "Just doing it," not waiting for favorable attitudes toward female leadership to emerge. They move forward when rejected and prefer the "I'll just do it myself" attitude when help is not offered or does not arrive.

The majority of the women surveyed lived in the northeast corridor of the country and were currently serving in the Methodist or Baptist traditions. Many of them were raised in denominations that limited female participation in prophetic leadership roles. They changed their denominational affiliations to increase their options for opportunity and growth.

The profile reveals that these women are college educated and actively taking courses to support their call into the gospel ministry. The majority have had some seminary training and/or are currently enrolled in one. One-third have already achieved advanced degrees in religious studies.

The women surveyed and interviewed were either ordained or just beginning denominational preparation towards ordination. Of those surveyed, 30 percent were already serving as pastors, and the majority were serving as associate ministers in local churches.

Those with seminary experience expressed that there was a lack of female-sensitive opportunities in their seminary experience. The desire for inclusiveness on the part of women in the ministry did not exclude their desire for courses and gender-specific learning experiences. If they could design their own seminary program, this group of women would include course work that reflects current contemporary ministry concerns. That desire nearly equaled the wish to study gender-specific issues. The women were interested in issues pertaining to ministry to the handicapped, teen pregnancy, spousal and sexual abuse, ministerial burnout, new innovations in ministry, proposal writing, and ministerial ethics.

Almost as many women wanted courses that were gender-related, such as sexism in the church, preaching from a female perspective, attitudes of men and women toward female clergy, the impact of physiological changes on women and their ministry, the balance of family and ministry, and female bonding. This group of women were also interested in experiences that enhanced, not eroded, relationships with their male counterparts. They wanted to relate effectively to men in ministry during this transition of paradigms until these opposing realities yielded a new partnership.

A woman in the pulpit represents a lot of changes for herself as well as for the congregation. She may represent the congregants' first experience of hearing a woman preach, teach, serve communion, or preside over rituals and board meetings. In interviews, the majority of the ministers expressed that their urge to grow was stronger than their resistance to change. As change agents themselves, they had taken college courses or courses related to ministry within the last three to five years. They preferred retreats over seminars and workshops as shared learning experiences.

MENTORS

Mentors play valuable roles in the lives of both men and women in the corporate and church communities. A mentor can help navigate the often-treacherous waters of spoken and unspoken rules and codes of behavior. A mentor can assist a protégé up the ladder of promotion, demystifying company and/or church politics. A mentor can get a protégé included in the right meeting, place her name before decision makers, have her résumé reviewed by the one who determines who is hired or fired, and share with her valuable insight and wisdom gathered over years of service.

Many women in business miss opportunities simply because they do not understand how offers are conveyed.[2] Women mistakenly believe that professional preparation is the only criterion for promotion or that hard work is always rewarded, for both men and women. They do not always know the power of the status quo or the unspoken rules of the work environment. Mentors can help.

Male as well as female mentors can be helpful. However, in trying to learn the political ropes, women must remember that male mentors often do not understand the rules of professional conduct for women.[3] What is good for the goose is not always good for the gander. Male leaders' mistakes may be overlooked, forgiven, or subject to appropriate reprimands. Female leaders' mistakes may receive the same treatment, but the women interviewed indicated that a mistake could be like a "sickness unto death" for them in local churches or denominational organizations. Some clergymen's indiscretions may be overlooked and/or forgiven. But clergywomen's indiscretions brand them, even taint their reputations, for a long time; they may become a hole from which it is difficult to climb out. The gossip about the same slips in judgment seem juicier and to travel farther when a female leader is involved. One of the interviewees said, "If you are doing right, you never have to worry about being caught wrong."

Marital discord, carelessness in moral conduct, and children trapped into society's sickness of drugs or alcohol are heavy burdens for anyone. When there is a female leader involved, the burden often weighs even heavier.

Yes, it is unfair! The same rules and standards should apply to both male and female clergy leaders. However, a congregation may tolerate a male minister who cannot keep his hands to himself or one who is a little free with women other than his wife. But that same congregation will have a low tolerance for a female minister who, as one sister-pastor said, "plays where she prays."

In fact, the general consensus of those interviewed was that if a clergywoman is too good looking, she is regarded suspiciously by other women and men. If she is committed to her ministry, then she must be unhappy at home. If she balances her work and home life, then she is neglecting her "call." If she looks too glamorous, then she is looking for extra male companionship. If she does not look at all glamorous, then she has no self-pride. If she dresses too well or lives too "high on the hog," then she must be stealing. If she does not live well enough, she is an embarrassment to God and the church. If she is single, than she must be scouting the congregation for a husband. If she is a married woman, she must either be playing the field or not taking care of her husband or children properly.

One male pastor, who travels internationally among several denominations, related that a woman in the ministry is in a difficult position. If she is too friendly with male peers, people feel that she wants something that does not belong to her. If she keeps her distance from the male preachers, then she is cold and calculating with a hard heart and no feelings.

More than 42 percent of the women in the study had a mentor, and the majority reported that they utilized both male and female mentors. They felt that mentors helped them gain the necessary clout for upward mobility, developing leadership skills, and accessibility to other decision makers.

The women indicated in their responses that their "sounding board" or "trusted other" with whom they could network and exchange ideas came from three different groups of people: friends, who could be either male or female; others in the ministry; and girlfriends. A friend may be either male or female; girlfriend denotes a greater female-friend intimacy within social context, more than professional. They dialogue with friends more than peers. The persons they least exchanged ideas with were denominational superiors, such as district superintendents, presiding elders, and bishops.

The ministers were able to name three other women to whom they looked upon as ministry role models. Among the women mentioned were: Rev. Cecelia Bryant of Akousa Ministries, Episcopal Supervisor of the Tenth Episcopal District (Texas) in the A.M.E. Church; Dr. Renita Weems Espinoza, author and professor at Vanderbilt School of Divinity; Dr. Prathia Hall Wynn, United Theological Seminary; Dr. Ann Lightner Fuller, pastor, Mt. Calvary A.M.E. Church; Dr. Suzan D. Johnson Cook, pastor, Mariners Temple Baptist Church; Rev. Debyii Thomas, associate minister, Hunter Memorial A.M.E. Church; Evangelist Jackie McCulloh of Brooklyn, New York; Rev. Corletta Harris-Vaughan, pastor, Full Gospel Baptist Church, Detroit Michigan; Dr. Ernestine Reems, pastor, Center of Hope Community Church, Oakland, California; Dr. Millicent Thompson, pastor, The Baptist Worship Center, Philadelphia; Dr. Ella Mitchell, author, United Theological Seminary; Dr. Jacquelyn Grant, ITC, Atlanta, Georgia; and Dr. Vashti McKenzie, pastor, Payne Memorial A.M.E. Church, Baltimore.

For the most part, participants indicated minister role models who served in their own region. The exception were those women who either had national preaching ministries or had authored popular books.

Some respondents reached beyond religious circles for role modes. The women most often mentioned were poet and author Maya Angelou, the late congresswoman Barbara Jordan, congresswoman Maxine Waters of California, and Marian Wright Edelman of the Children's Defense Fund.

In a crisis, however, the women did not consult human resources at all. They sought comfort in a divine presence, listing either God or Jesus Christ. They accomplished this through the spiritual disciplines of prayer and fasting. The creative flow of ideas was shared with other human beings, but crises and the tension, stress, and anxiety that accompanies them were shared in dialogue with God. They shared their successes with humans and their problems with the Divine.

One of the women reflected that in times of crisis Esther prayed and fasted to God for three days with great results. David found strength to do battle from his conversations with God. Moses found answers to his many dilemmas of the wilderness experience while in private consultation with God.

The positive side of this response is that women are able to connect to a higher source beyond themselves during a crisis. The negative is that it promotes a sense of isolationism—the "I feel like I'm in it by myself" attitude. Many women suffer in silence. After they "take it to the Lord in prayer," many do not ever share the struggle with others who can serve as rich resources and sources of advice.

A majority of the women entered ministry from vocations that were not related to religious groups. Ministry was a second career with most of them, having come from careers in education, administration, management, social work, medicine, finance, and legal fields. The respondents indicated that they learned organizational skills, human relations, crisis intervention, analysis of issues, and counseling from their previous vocations. They also indicated that they were able to transfer these skills to their current roles as ministers. One minister wrote that she gained confidence to speak to large groups of people on her job, working with a wide range of personalities and "keeping cool in times of crisis." Another minister responded that her previous employment gave her insight into the spiritual and emotional needs of individuals. A full-time associate minister wrote that she learned valuable clerical and managerial experience, planning, and decision-making skills in her previous vocation, which help her tremendously in ministry.

Even though the majority of the women currently serve as pastors and associate ministers, they still work in vocations outside of the ministry. They do this primarily for economic reasons. Many of them serve as pastors and associates in low-paid and unpaid positions. They continued to work in other careers out of necessity.

Some of the clergywomen responded that they were part-time ministers. That is, many work a portion of the week in their church or ministry and spend the majority of their time working elsewhere. This, too, is primarily an economic decision. A few of the women working two careers were quick to note that they work full-time in part-time positions in their respective churches.

The women were given three types of behaviors to choose from in the questionnaire and the interviews. They were aggressive, assertive, and passive. They could indicate which mostly applied to them.

The intent was see basically how the majority of the women viewed themselves. In other male-dominated vocations, two generalization about female temperament occur. One is that women are considered "too soft," "too emotional," "too nice," "too sweet," or "too passive" as leaders in professional arenas including the church. The other generalization is that women who are considered aggressive are often accused of being "too mannish" or "a witch" (or something else that rhymes with it).

One minister interviewed shared privately that first her congregation mistook her "being nice" as a sign of weakness. She had to demonstrate constantly that being nice did not mean she that could not make hard and tough decisions when necessary. In a similar way, another minister said that others treated her too much "like one of the boys." She was accused of being too "arrogant" while young male ministers were being described as just "ambitious."

The vast majority of the women saw themselves as assertive. Only a few described themselves as either aggressive or passive.

In order to uncover some measure of satisfaction or dissatisfaction of women in the ministry, the ministers were asked if they could start all over again, what would they do. The majority of the women indicated that they would not change anything, not even the hardships and problems because "they forced me to think sharper and plan better." One pastor of a metropolitan church, in her mid-thirties, stated that "I wouldn't even change the bumps in the road. The bumps helped to make me a better pastor." "Learn the organization and polity of the church as it relates to my work in ministry," wrote one full-time associate minister.

The ministers were also asked if they could make improvements in their personal lives, what they would be. The majority indicated a desire to improve numerous things, including learning to say "no," self-discipline, greater sensitivity, and taking time to develop sister-friend relationships. There were concerns expressed about taking better care of health, personal finances, and family. The ministers also mentioned avoiding "people with no common sense," "people who bring me down," and "people who try to limit me and my ministry." One full-time pastor of a rural church stated "I'm tired of all the people who keep saying no to my femaleness, my Blackness and my ministry. Sometimes I feel as if the whole world is against me!"

The historical perspectives reveal that women in the ministry struggled against social paradigms just to respond to the call of God. But how do women handle rejection now in the twenty-first century?

A majority of the women indicated that before responding to rejection of their leadership, they seek guidance and direction from God. Prayer, for many of them, was the primary method of seeking help quickly. They also indicated that they would take time to evaluate the critic and the circumstances before determining a course of action. "I try to evaluate my position and the motive of the critic before responding," said one veteran minister.

Very few women indicated that they had allowed rejection to impede them. Their responses included such reactions as "continuing to do the work," "moving forward anyhow," "shifting gears," "asking questions in love," and making attempts to dialogue with the other persons.

Some of the women admitted that there were times when the constant rejection "got to them," and they took the rejection personally, spoke harshly, or walked away angrily, only later to feel stressed out about the incident.

Many respondents shared "war stories" about past events when the opposition rose to reject their ministry or leadership. Numerous overt and covert things had been done by ministers of the gospel as well as the laity.

"I was invited to preach for a women's day afternoon service," said one minister. "When the other male ministers were escorted to the pastor's office, I was taken to a seat in the secretary's office. The usual courtesies extended to visiting preachers were not given." She indicated that the attitude of the pastor toward her was cold and indifferent. The minister sat in the front row during the entire service while the other preachers sat in the pulpit. Instead of being invited up to the pulpit, she was told to preach from a lectern on the floor. Another minister whispered to her sarcastically that she should go home rather than stand being insulted that way. "I ignored the comment and preached anyway. God was going to fight this battle for me," she said. "People shouted and cried during the sermon, and many people came forward responding to the call for Christian discipleship. The pastor sat amazed in silence. I never let these things bother me," she concluded. "If no one else is for me, I know God is!"

Another pastor noted that many times church members respond to female leadership negatively because it is a new experience for them. Once they get to know you and see the gifts that God has given you, church members really do not care whether you are male or female, only whether you "can deliver the mail." "By the time you take them through the Old and New Testament evidence of God's called-out women, most members and ministers begin to help you instead of hindering you," said an associate minister.

The ministers overwhelmingly refused to be stymied by men or other women rejecting their female leadership. Those responding indicated behaviors that were firm, confident, and persevering. "The Bible and Lord, being my helper," wrote one student minister.

Only a few ministers communicated that they are now less defensive about their call to the gospel ministry. All of the women indicated a distaste for those women wounded in the struggle who espoused a gospel of pain and hate. They do not feel that one must justify one's call every time one preaches. Only a few interviewed said they had never experienced rejection or opposition to their ministry or leadership.

When asked specifically what their response would be if a local church board vetoed their proposal, the majority of the women indicated an active response. The intent of the question was to see how the women acted or reacted to a nongender crisis. The majority of the ministers interviewed noted that they would resubmit the proposal for future consideration and/or go on to the next issue. Many said they would be ready with a "plan B, or C, even D if plan A failed to get enough votes." As indicated earlier, in a crisis, the women also indicated that they would "pray about it" and "leave it the hands of the God."

The majority of the ministers enjoyed "being in charge." They were comfortable in a leadership role. Only a minute number found themselves "in charge" and not liking it. A majority of them adopted the do-it-yourself approach to leadership. There was an indication that they were pressured into this style or simply chose it because of congregational attitudes. The style was either a reactive response to having received little or no help or support in local churches, or it was simply the style that worked best for them.

Rev. Carolyn Jones, the first female associate minister at Crenshaw Presbyterian Church, wrote in a book edited by Lyle E. Schaller that there was a lot of the do-it-yourselfer in her, which was a surprise to the people at her church. She has subsequently changed her approach to reflect more of Ephesians 4, "the equipping the saints for the work of the ministry."[4]

One associate minister, serving in a small congregation for four years, said that she found it easier to "just do it myself." In that way, she did not have to depend on the whims of others or have her efforts jeopardized by others who did not fully advocate her success.

Although a majority of the ministers indicated a do-it-yourself preference, almost an equal number indicated that they preferred to "delegate responsibilities." They "networked the power-base" of the congregation and "shared the load" of power and responsibilities. "If Jesus needed twelve to help him, I certainly need others to help me," said one pastor. "I'm able to increase the effectiveness of the ministry by empowering the laity to serve. I don't make it a women's thing but a Jesus thing in my congregation. They are not helping me, they are serving God!"

The ministers questioned were given descriptive words so that they could choose the ones that best described their relationship to ministry. The words were *wife* and *husband*; *Titanic*; *Apollo*; *mother* and *daughter/son*; *sister* and *brother*; *horse and carriage*; and *locomotive* and *caboose*. Each of these words gives a mental picture that could possibly reveal where a particular woman is in relationship to her work. For example, if a woman describes her ministry as *Apollo,* it may indicate that she feels her ministry is taking off like a rocket. When a minister uses the term *Titanic,* it may mean that the ministry is sinking like the ill-fated ship. The *wife* and *husband* words evoke images of a ministry with close intimate relationships. The relationship exists because they mutually agree in a covenant-type commitment.

The *mother* and *daughter/son* terms present a maternal image. In this description, the minister is the mother. Her ministry is the child, to be nurtured, loved, and raised to maturity. The *sister/brother* description is one where siblings form a partnership. They did not choose each other but by "family" ties are working together.

The *horse and carriage* description presents an image that the minister is pulling her work along. The *locomotive* gives the impression that the minister is out in front of this ministry, and the *caboose* represents the people or ministry program. The horse-and-carriage image gives an impression of plodding along, while the locomotive represents power and strength.

The majority of the women used relational terms to describe themselves and their ministry. The terms most frequently chosen, in equal numbers, were *sister/brother* and *mother/daughter/son*. The second most commonly chosen term was *husband/wife*. Very few chose the other images. No one chose the Titanic.

When women and men are committed to a cause greater than themselves, they tend to give more than 100 percent. Many women responded in the survey that they saw to the needs of their congregants, church, and family first. Their personal needs were left for last. On an average, the majority of the women spent only one or two hours per week on personal needs. The majority indicated that they spent at least fifteen minutes per day for personal devotion outside of sermon or Bible study preparation. One minister wrote in big letters there is never "enough time." Taking time for personal needs contributes to a person's well-being. The ministers indicated that when they did take the time out for themselves, they had no guilty feelings at all. "Everybody in the world knows I deserve some time for me," said one busy pastor of a 200-member congregation.

The majority of the respondents had developed a regular relaxation routine. They engaged in a variety of activities that were either physical, spiritual, or solitary. The women exercised, bowled, rode bicycles, or skated. They also engaged in solitary activities such as listening to music, reading, taking hot bubble baths or long walks, or just being alone. Their spiritual relaxation included prayer, meditation, and reading religious literature. The women also indicated that they relaxed by socializing with friends.

Many times when the demands of the ministry and family increase, hobbies and vacations that refresh the body and mind are abandoned. Sixty percent of the ministers did indicate that they actively participated in personal hobbies, mostly in the area of the arts, dance, sports, and reading. "I dig my frustrations out in my garden every weekend that I can," wrote one associate minister. "I love to cook. So I cook for my family, friends, and the church," said another. "If I can find a quiet stream once in a while to make believe I'm going to catch fish, I'd be a happy hobbyist," said a pastor of an urban congregation.

These women, who only spend a few hours on themselves each week, also rarely took vacations. A majority of them had taken vacations within the last three years; however, their vacations were linked to church conferences, denominational events, and revivals and retreats, where they had an active role to play. "You learn how to go early or stay a few days late," wrote one pastor. "You may work like a horse, but at least you get a break from the daily routine." One seminarian listed her honeymoon five years ago as her last vacation.

PROFILE OF THE AFRICAN AMERICAN WOMAN IN MINISTRY

There is a profile of an African American woman in ministry that emerges from the 164 women surveyed and interviewed. This profile emerges from the compilation of the majority responses to the twenty-eight questions and statements.

The average participating woman in ministry is an ordained associate minister, planning on a pastoral ministry. She is a baby boomer between the ages of forty and forty-nine years. She is a college graduate with some seminary experience. She views education as the doorway to advancement, opportunity, and ordination in her denomination. Therefore, she has actively taken courses in religious studies for the past three to five years.

The women surveyed and interviewed have explicit opinions about what was lacking in their ministerial training. They feel they lacked gender-specific opportunities such as courses specifically geared to women in preaching, ministry, and church history. They also wanted "more work with the Bible" and the "practical aspects of day-to-day ministry."

If they could design a leadership training program for women in the ministry, the majority of the women wanted two areas to be included specifically: contemporary ministry issues and women's issues.

The profile of this group of ministers indicates that they are independent, in charge, and liking it. They are being mentored both by other women and men in the ministry. They admire other clergywomen more than secular women in the areas of administration, organization, singing, praying, preaching, and teaching.

They are largely a confident group of ministers who count on their faith in God to help them handle the challenges of ministry. They are also concerned about the development of their own spiritual resources and improving their personal lives "to work smarter, we are already working harder."

The pressure to prove their competence often pressures them to isolate themselves in times of crisis. In spite of stress, anxiety, and exhaustion, they work hard not to show the struggles they endure.

The portrait painted by these ministers reveals that they share ideas readily with friends. But in crises they find comfort and solace in God. When their leadership is rebuffed, they find strength in God. They pray before taking any action in the presence of critics and opposition. They are not stymied when nongender-based crises arise over their programs in the boardroom. They simply pray, actively move to resubmit, or move on.

The average minister is working three jobs: one at the church, one in another vocation, and one at home. She does this primarily for economic reasons. She spends one or more hours per week on her own personal needs. She takes her vacation in conjunction with religious responsibilities. When she does take time for herself, she does not feel guilty about it.

The ministry is a second career to this group of women. They have transferred skills learned in previous vocations or current ones to the ministry.

The women favor two types of leadership stances: "do it yourself" and "let's do it together." They see themselves as primarily assertive. They engage in a relationship with their ministry as brother and sister—two siblings together, not by choice but by divine direction.

The shared experiences of the 164 women who participated were often very personal. These glimpses into their lives were enlightening and can be used for further dialogue among the men and women of the clergy

WOMANIST LEADERSHIP STYLE RESPONSE

A womanist leadership style response was developed from the profile of the 164 women surveyed and interviewed. This response takes into consideration the historical, contemporary, and biblical role models plus the compilation of shared experiences with clergywomen in workshops, seminars, and retreats over the past fifteen years. This womanist style response utilizes a theoretical leadership framework. The model includes distinctive African American attitudes plus those characteristics found in Eurocentric models.

It may be useful here to review briefly the four basic leadership styles found in Charles Keating's *Leadership Book* and discussed in chapter 6. The first style is "high relationship and low task." This "country club" leader gives more attention to the relationships of a group and less attention to the work. The second style is "high task and low relation." This leader is more direct, concerned more about the work than the personalities involved. The third style is "high task and high relationship." It is characterized by nurturing leader behavior with clearly defined goals. The fourth style is "low task and low relationship." This is a low-impact style, in both relationships and work. These first six style responses are distinguished by the quantity of task and relationship involved.

The second set of four leader styles are developed from African American culture and experience. These are not the only possible groupings of leader behaviors; they are just the groupings chosen for this book. The ten leader styles are visible in various economic classes including low, middle, and upper. The categories are also visible in various educational and social levels within the African American communities.

A leader may have some or all the characteristics of a particular grouping. A leader may also use one style as a dominant style and switch to others in different or difficult circumstances. Some women move easily from one style to another and find that their style is actually a combination of several groupings. These leader styles can also be applied to African American woman leaders in other arenas as well the clergy. Some of these leader behaviors can be discerned by watching male African American leaders as well.

SISTER GIRLFRIEND

The *sister girlfriend* is usually an active member of any group, work site, or church she belongs to. She thrives on communal feeling and friendship. Her secret of leader success is in the network of friends she makes inside and outside of the church. *Sister girlfriend* works hard to build a collegial atmosphere. She is everybody's friend. Hell for her is to be alone or to have to do anything alone. She enjoys being the center of every group or congregation. Her office and her home are filled with people working, or those who just happen to drop by for a chat and chew.

A popular leader, *sister girlfriend* spends lots of time with her congregants outside the church in social activities. She could be called the "clique princess," because she is in one wherever she goes.

Everyone knows her. Those who work with her often see her as "sister" or "best friend" rather than boss, supervisor, or pastor. Her door is always open, and the telephone is always busy. She has time for everyone, sometimes to her own detriment. The group dominates the achievement of goals for this leader.

She is a great person to work with/under, but how much will really be accomplished? Work tends to be sporadic. What is important to *sister girlfriend* is not what she does but who she is with. This orientation is the highest in personal relationships and lowest in task.

THE QUEEN

The *queen* leader does not merely take charge, she rules over her organization or church. She reigns supreme, with full authoritative power, bowing only to God. The *queen* is in control of everything and everyone around her. There are no "freethinkers" or "self-starters" in her court. Everyone must wait for the royal command to start and finish.

She could best be described as a royal "benevolent dictator." You do not just drop in to see the *queen*; you must wait to be summoned. Until then, you had better be doing your job, or "off with your head!"

Her letters are written like royal dictates, and her memos are more like commands. She is a direct leader, who orders things to be done rather than asks. She is more than in charge and loves every minute of it.

This leader "takes no stuff off of anyone"—after all she is not the "clique princess" like the "sister girlfriend" but the *queen*. Anyone who fails to recognize the rule and sovereignty of this leader usually only makes that mistake once. There is rarely a second chance. There is no doubt as to who she is and what she can do, for everyone recognizes her eminence.

The *queen* leader focuses her attention on the activities of her congregation or organization. The wants and needs of the body revolve around the wants, needs, and ideas of the *queen*. This leader's achievement rate is high and her accomplishments are many. She often suffers from poor or strained relations with coworkers, but followers shout "Long live the queen!" This leader reflects the high-task and low-relationship style.

MAMA

Mama is just what every church needs. She has everyone organized, from the youngest to the oldest. Everyone has some responsibility in the church. Tasks are assigned, and *Mama* lovingly sees each one through.

Her church is bustling with achievement because no one can refuse *Mama* anything. Who can say no when *Mama* asks you and makes you feel like you are the only one in the world who can get the job done. Then you check back with *Mama* when you finish, because she might have something else for you to do.

You can never say no to her, because she does so much for you. *Mama* goes beyond the call of duty, extending her reach outside of the church to take care of all her "children." She adopts everyone without regard to race, creed, color, national origin, or age. You can be fifty years old and still be one of *Mama's* children.

She is "in your business"—your love life, marriage, and the raising of your children. Without even realizing what you are doing, you tell *Mama* all your problems. She will dry your tears, give you money, reprimand you, and nurture you into doing a great job.

Mama is about "equipping the saints for service." She raises her congregation the way she would raise her own children. She teaches and nurtures them into mature behavior. She gives them responsibility and expects them to handle it. This leadership style leader is high in both the task and relationship dimensions.

WISE WOMAN

The *wise woman* is the sage. She does not always hang with the crowd, does not reign over her responsibilities, is not always buddy-buddy with everyone, and she does not act as a mother figure. This leader is able to apply gained knowledge and experience. Her wisdom can be legendary, and everyone seeks her advice and counsel.

She has a sense of a divine call, and it shows. She tends not to get trapped into gender arguments or gender defense. She seems to transcend cultural and societal biases to perform her responsibilities, not as a *female* pastor or *female* minister, but as a pastor or a minister. She moves with deliberate action, and her purposes are clear. Others are inspired to follow her lead.

The *wise woman* is called the Zoe in some African traditions. The Zoe is the wise keeper of the traditions of the people. She is the transmitter of heritage and history. She is the teacher of young and old alike. They come to her to find out if a plan, project, program, or idea is in keeping with their traditions. The Zoe then dispenses advice.

Our *wise woman* may also function in the same manner. Her secret of success comes from her ability to give wise counsel competently and to inspire others to follow clearly defined goals. She is a low-relationship, low-task leader.

SAPPHIRE

The name Sapphire may jog a few pre-boomer memories. She was a character on the radio and television program "Amos and Andy" a few generations ago. Of all the things you could say about Sapphire, she was without question a "three-D" woman—determined, direct, and demanding. The name of this type of leader was also selected because, just as the gemstone is distinguished by its strong colors, *Sapphire* is noted for being a strong leader. Just as the gem stands out even when surrounded by diamonds and pearls, this leader stands out in any crowd.

Not the queen, clique princess, mother, or sage of corporate America or the church, *Sapphire* is often labeled as too aggressive and too ambitious. But she is merely misunderstood. Her sense of duty and responsibility fuels her determined attitude. She works hard at whatever she does, with little patience for those who do not share her sense of duty and dedication.

Sapphire's perfectionism is the reason why others accuse her of being too demanding. She is just trying to do the job right, the first time and every time. Some leaders of this type are workaholics: they come early and leave late; they are over-involved, over-stretched, over-stressed, and enjoy being over everything. A direct and confrontational leader, *Sapphire* doesn't have time for finesse and doesn't perceive the value of tact. She cuts to the chase and goes for the jugular every time. She deals directly with those in positions of authority. She spends little time with and on the middlemen or middle management.

Sapphire is goal-conscious, a quintessential high-task, low-relationship leader. You expect her to speak when spoken to in casual encounters, but she doesn't always. It is not that she is ignoring you; her mind is on her work. She doesn't speak to you simply because she doesn't see or hear you.

People always seem to have a lot to say about *Sapphire*. The determined, direct, and demanding way she works fuels the gossip mill. Congregants may complain about her drive and toughness. But they tend to respect her talent for getting things done. In fact, when people want something done, they will call *Sapphire* every time.

Sapphire is an in-charge sister. She is not apprehensive about putting her hands on her hips or putting you in your place. She knows how to "work her neck" and work you at the same time. Don't look for her to cry when hurt, at least not publicly, but underneath her tough exterior is a softer interior. She is not a "soft touch," but scratch the surface a little and there *is* a heart under there.

FINESSA

While *Sapphire* is rough around the edges, *Finessa* is as smooth as it gets in her approach to leadership. She put the "f" in finesse. She'll lead her church or organization until the engines don't just run, they purr. She is as fierce as a lion, but doesn't have to roar. She purrs her commands, directions, and questions. Honey drips from her lips and send coworkers scrambling to get things done. She can charm a snake out of its hiss. She can talk you into doing what you said you wouldn't do, take you where you don't want to go, and get you to give what you said you wouldn't give. And you'll end up thanking her for doing it, she's that smooth.

Finessa works hard. She places equal value on achieving her goals and using good people skills. Her leadership approach is nondirective, with a way of moving people and things around like pieces on a chessboard. The group, company, or church will accomplish much and the people may enjoy the ride.

Don't be fooled by her polish. Many are caught off-guard by her finesse. She may never raise her voice, pound on the table, or appear threatening. But *Finessa* has claws and knows how to use them. She can cut you so fast and smooth that you won't know it until you're on the floor bleeding to death.

As classy as she is smooth, this leader prefers the best, and sometimes even the best is not good enough. Some *Finessa*s are at home with expensive cars, expensive clothes, expensive restaurants, and expensive environments. Whenever the powers-that-be need to impress with an uptown style, they send for *Finessa*.

She is often accused of being stuck up or snooty. Some may even accuse her of thinking of herself more highly than she ought or thinking she's better than everyone. But *Finessa* is not bothered by the critics. She is too much of a class act to dignify their comments with a response.

Sapphire may be described as a hard woman working harder and a hard act to follow. *Finessa* has been able to aptly disguise her toughness. She is best described as the "iron fist in the velvet glove."

The next set of leader behaviors stem from some of the cultural and social experiences of African Americans.

LIBERATIONIST

The *liberationist* is a leader who espouses the ideals of liberation thought, philosophy, and theology in everything. Liberation is not merely a focus of energy in this direction; it is an obsession. It is not just one of several issues she may be concerned about; it is the dominant or only issue.

This leader espouses the ideals of liberation which include economic empowerment, nationalism, and civil rights. She involves other individuals and the congregation in activities that push for the liberation of African Americans and other oppressed groups, including women.

She sees racism in everything and suspects that every governmental act or corporate decision might be racist based. The burden of oppression and the quest for liberation, rather than personal relationships and other tasks, are the motivations of this leader.

AFRICENTRIC

The *Africentric* leader is immediately recognized by her dress and hairstyle, which reflect an intense Africentric view. This leader may be known for wearing traditional or contemporary African dress. Her hair may be braided, or worn in cornrows or dreadlocks. She may wear kente stripes, celebrate Kwanzaa, and decorate her home and her church with African artwork and artifacts.

This leader has rediscovered her roots in Africa and desires others to know their rich heritage. She may develop worship, teaching, and ministry around an African motif. She may even inspire others to a consciousness and concern for the Motherland, Africa.

CHAMELEON

Just as the ancient lizard protectively changes colors to suit its environment, so does this leader. She changes her ethnic attitude and orientation protectively to suit the surrounding work environment.

The *chameleon* is comfortable around a variety of ethnic groups. When in Rome, she is able to do as Romans do, as well as do what the Bushmen do in South Africa. She is bilingual—she can rap with the girls in the hood and dialogue with intellectuals at Spelman College. She is comfortable with yuppies, buppies, and home girls. She does not have to cook greens, neckbones, cornbread, or pig's feet, but knows how to go to the soul food restaurant to take home her culture if necessary. She is comfortable in high-priced and high-profile positions. She can sip cappuccino with the best of them. But she will still go back to the neighborhood to get her hair done—her perm and/or weave.

This leader is the master of flexibility. She knows how to blend in, fit in to get in. She knows how to get along to go along up the denominational ladder. Her motivation is not by relationship or tasks but by her ability to change to suit any cultural environment.

YO, BABY, YO

This last leader is a woman who came up the hard way. She had few opportunities and fewer advantages in life. She would have pulled herself up by her bootstraps if she had had the boots. *Yo*'s skills were honed on the street. She learned to depend on no one but herself. She learned to trust only what she can see, test, and verify for herself. All her life she has gotten by on her wit, street knowledge, and common sense.

This leader has excellent survival skills. She has worked too hard and has gone too far to lose whatever ground or position she has gained. When working situations call for responses that are "down and dirty," she can scrap with the best of them. She does not back away from a fight. She knows how to fight for what she wants and how to protect her "turf" or church.

Her street skills are sharp throughout her leadership career. They may be conditioned and camouflaged by educational and other experiences but are never lost. The motivation of this Daughter of the Struggle may be measurable on both task and relationship dimensions, but she derives her style from her experience on the street.

Chapter eight

Ten Commandments for African American Women in the Ministry

TEN COMMANDMENTS FOR African American Women in the Ministry are a collection of leadership strategies offered as a resource for African American clergywomen, in particular, and clergywomen in general. This collection is a pool of advice solicited from women actively involved in a variety of ministries nationally. These commandments may be considered groups of basic leader laws or a code of leader conduct. They are not absolute principles, but many of them are consistent and constant in a variety of ministry environments.

This collection of commandments may be used by other women as a guiding resource of advice and counsel in their own ministry. Many of the 164 women surveyed and interviewed expressed that they felt a sense of isolation. Many served in communities as the sole woman or one of few women. Ministerial collegiality and support were all but absent.

It is hoped that this list of hints and tips will serve as written mentor advice by clergy, especially those in isolated circumstances. These lists can also be used as a teaching tool for both men and women in the ministry—especially those just taking on the yoke of the gospel plow. They are a good place to begin ministerial dialogue among peers.

Originally, thirty-eight women compiled a list of "Ten Thou Shalls" and "Ten Thou Shall Nots." Additionally, of the one hundred women previously interviewed, fifty-five submitted a list of "Ten Thou Shalls." The majority were associate ministers and pastors in the Methodist and Baptist traditions. Fifty percent had advanced degrees in religious studies. They submitted 880 suggested commandments.

Since the original Ten Commandments are a series of absolute principles or basic laws of human social conduct given by God, the Ten Commandments for Women in the Ministry is not to be considered on a par with God's revelation recorded in Exodus 21. They should, however, be considered valuable women's leadership beliefs.

These Ten Commandments are basic leadership tactics. The ministers shared the advice they learned from their own struggles and experience in the ministry. They willingly shared with the hope that the suggestions might help another "Daughter of Thunder."

TEN COMMANDMENTS FOR AFRICAN AMERICAN CLERGYWOMEN

1. THOU SHALL BE PREPARED

The burden of proof for women in the ministry is heavy. Women reported in the interviews that they had to work harder to prove themselves better than the best male at the same position. They had to be not only qualified but overqualified to be even considered.

Many times congregants and superiors looked for the slightest error or defect to discredit a woman's work, leadership, or ministry. The pressure to be "on target" was incredible, many of the women reported.

As a result, a minister must be prepared spiritual, emotionally and physically to serve God. A minister must be prepared, like a Girl Scout, to do her best, to preach, teach, and serve, trying never to disappoint a congregation. A spiritually hungry person needs to be fed by the undershepherd. Sheep will go where they can get a meal; if you are unprepared to cook, then dish and serve spiritual meals.

Some women's struggle and pain seduce them to ascribe to the psychology of failure. Their expectations of achievement are low; they do not expect to make it. When the doors finally open, they are often not prepared to do the job. Thou shall be prepared, and thou shall be competent! Preparation includes but is not limited to theological education; personal and spiritual disciplines; developing a support team of mentors, family, friends, and peers; and gaining work-site experiences in churches, seminaries, hospitals, prisons, and other ministries. Preparation also means being ready to preach "in season and out of season." It means establishing regular times to write sermons, prepare lesson plans for Bible studies or Sunday school, read resource materials, and engage in personal prayer. Congregations tend to have little patience with preachers who "wing it" week after week, or with those who fail to seek God for a vision for the mission and ministry. It may be trite but it is true: If you fail to plan, you are planning to fail.

"When you take on the superficial techniques of manipulating people without being competent or skillful, others will soon see what you are doing and will not follow your leadership," said a pastor and denominational leader.

2. THOU SHALL BE A TEAM PLAYER

It is very difficult to get far alone in this world and in ministry. The sun still shines on the "Lone Ranger" leader, but her days are getting shorter. It behooves a minister to learn how to play the game. This includes building relationships with other team members, playing with and not against team members, supporting other team members in their ambitions, and learning how to play your position well. It also includes learning how to be the team leader, coaching the players, and playing ball (punt, pass, and kick; pitch, hit, and run; or stitch, weave, and spin) if necessary.

You will have an opportunity to "rust out" instead of "wear out" when you are also able to assemble a championship team of staff and volunteers in the church. This team should consist of men and women in the church, who work with you and not against you in the service of God. They should want to be on the team and want to play on your side. This is a critical issue, because many want to be on the team but they do not like the coach/pastor or coach/associate minister. Team members should be supportive of the team leader. They should understand the mission and ministry of the church and be committed to its success. Let all others "play" elsewhere. "Just because they belong to the church, doesn't mean they support women in the ministry," said one pastor. "They want to be you or to do you, not help you."

3. THOU SHALL NETWORK

The minister's work is never done, but do connect with other men and women in the ministry. It is in collegiality that alliances are formed which may eventually enhance your ministry and stimulate cooperative efforts in your community. It is in collegiality that ideas, information, and advice are shared. It is in collegiality that support can be garnered for activities of the local church. A lot can be learned just by observing others in the fellowship.

Your network should include connection with a variety of persons within the church, the denomination, and other faith traditions. It is wise to network with other women in leadership positions for mutual support and encouragement. A cooperative spirit among community leaders is also needed, including those in government, education, and civic concerns, which may be a source of support previously untapped.

4. Thou Shall Be Accountable

It is wise for any leader to exercise responsible behavior towards those who look to you for support, service and help. The beatitudes of accountability include:

- Be financially accountable to officers and members, even if they do not require it. Trust is not easily regained once it is lost.
- Be spiritually accountable to God and to those who are placed in your care. Personal devotion is as important as sermon and Bible study preparation.
- Be accountable to denominational supervisors or those who serve above you. Even if you have trouble respecting the individual, do respect the office.
- Be accountable to your family. Your, spouse, children, parents, and significant others are the Jerusalem to whom you shall be Jesus' witness first (Acts 1:8). What joy would there be in gaining the whole world for Jesus and losing your family?
- Be an example. Let others see you applying the word of God to your life inside and outside of the church.

5. Thou Shall Empower Others

One of the best examples of empowering leadership is Jesus Christ. He used a methodology of teaching (Mark 10:1; Luke 11:1; Matt. 5; Mark 9:33–36) demonstrating (Mark 9:14–32; Matt. 4:23–24), setting an example for others (John 13:15–17) and then letting them do it (Matt. 10:1–20, 28:19–20). It worked for Jesus, and it can work for leaders today, too.

Jesus empowered the twelve and others, and through them turned the world upside down. The disciples were not distinguished community leaders who wielded power and influence in Palestine. They did not hold academic positions; nor were they known for exceptional intellectual achievement. They were not persons of prestige in the social community. They did not have any recognizable achievement in the religious community.

They were ordinary people who were empowered by an extraordinary Savior to do extraordinary things. That same power is available today. Help others to become involved. The harvest is plentiful, and we need more laborers.

6. THOU SHALL USE SOUND MANAGEMENT PRINCIPLES AND TECHNIQUES

Major portions of church responsibility are business-oriented. Learn basic business procedures, read about new management techniques, and adapt what is useful in the administration of the church.

Learn what you can about finances. That does not mean that you should earn an M.B.A. (But it wouldn't hurt!) What it does mean is that you may need to be able to at least recognize a balance sheet, understand budgeting procedures, and maybe even know the difference between a debit and a credit.

If you are not talented in that area, gather those around you who are. One of the myths in ministry is that ministers must know everything. They must be experts in finance, plumbing, construction, architectural design, systems management, waste control, and hymnology, plus preaching, teaching, and praying.

Moses was a great leader but struggled with a lot of management problems. He had problems with personnel (Num. 12), water and food resources (Exod. 16–17), crowd control (Exod. 18), and morale (Exod. 32). Aaron was a good manager but lacked leadership, the ability of doing the right things (Exod. 32).

Moses could lead, and Aaron could manage. Moses had a special God-connection, and Aaron had the vocabulary. Moses was an outsider with a history, and Aaron was an insider with human connections. Each was empowered by God. Each empowered the other. Together, they made a great team.

7. Thou Shall Be Committed to the Servant Leadership Style of Management, Exemplified by Jesus Christ

Jesus Christ is our example of the servant-style leadership. An overwhelming number of the responses indicate that, for women in ministry, the servant leadership style was the ideal. Whether one has a "queen," "Mama," or "wise woman" style, some of the servant style must be included. A minister comes to serve rather than to be served (John 13:16). If one desires to be the leader, one must not lord it over others but first be a servant (Matt. 20:25–28). The towel and the responsibility to wash feet at the door are to be desired over the title. This is the example that Jesus set (John 13:16).

Many women are culturally raised to be the caretakers and nurturers of others including family members, children, and spouses. This training is an asset for pastoral work and similar to the transforming servant style of Jesus.

8. Thou Shall Pursue Continuing Education and Personal Development in Order to Provide Quality Leadership

Ministers must be determined to do their best as leaders. This means strengthening skills and abilities beyond the ordination process and the seminary. Workshops, retreats, seminars, and course work in related fields are encouraged; and most certainly ministers must read, read, read.

A leader's value is the ability to recognize the right things to do while the manager's value is doing things right. The key that unlocks the door to recognition of those ideas is continuing education.

"Thou shall not remain uninformed, and thou shall know everything there is to know," said a pastor. "Ask questions, study resources, and know more Bible."

A minister must be concern about professional development and personal development. Growing, reaching, stretching, challenging the process, and taking risks are the marks of most leaders. These activities should occur in the personal life of the minister who is setting an example for a congregation that is also growing and maturing.

9. Thou Shall Develop, Pursue, and Establish a Bible-Centered Ethics and Ethos in All Areas of Ministry

Leadership is an important motif in the Old and New Testaments. Leaders were so important that God became personally involved. Samson's parents were instructed on how the future judge was to be raised (Judg. 13:13). Older siblings were passed over in favor of the youngest, a shepherd boy, to be Israel's king (1 Sam. 16:1–13). Esther was chosen within the enemy's camp (Esther 4:14) while a woman with a suspicious lifestyle was selected wellside and Mary graveside to carry the news about the Christ (John 4:27–42; Mark 9:10–11; Matt. 28:9–10).

In the New Testament, the distinctions of race, class, and gender are erased by the universal blood and love of an equal-opportunity Savior. It does not matter if you are not born a Levite, a son of Aaron, without blemishes, Jewish, or male; the Bible says that your sons and daughters shall prophesy (Joel 28; Acts 2).

The Bible is also filled with truths about human resources, family matters, and other essentials for a Christian lifestyle. The minister has an opportunity to teach and guide her beloved community in demonstrating "how it ought to be done," said one associate minister.

10. Thou Shall Be Accessible to Christ and to Those You Are Called to Serve

"Thou shall spend time with the people," said a suburban pastor. "Thou shall enjoy, be stimulated and available to both lay persons and staff. Thou shall be a good listener and respond to what you hear," said another suburban pastor.

A minister has the unique opportunity to see members at their best and at their worse. A minister has the unique opportunity to participate in the best and the worst times of a person's life. The minister is there for the major events of a person's life, such as birth, youth, marriage, and death. A minister rejoices with a congregant over achievements and offers her shoulder to lean on in hard times.

A minister-leader must try not to neglect the management function of tending sheep. Similar to a physician on call, the minister is sometimes awakened in the night just to pray with a distraught member. Other times, when the minister's body is weak, she is called to do hospital visitation, funeral services, weddings, and even Sabbath-morning responsibilities. A majority of the congregation may never call; but have office hours, if applicable, anyway. Be available by telephone for personal consultation. The personal touch goes a long way in building community.

The minister plays a significant role beyond corporate worship, teaching, and study. The women polled overwhelmingly said "remember to be available." But they also noted that there are times when a minister must have rest, relaxation, and recreation. There are times when a minister must say "no" to member requests.

Some leadership strategies shared in the survey may be classified as womanist in nature. They make or imply specific gender references. The following list elaborates on Ten Womanist Commandments for clergy.

TEN WOMANIST COMMANDMENTS FOR CLERGY

1. THOU SHALL NOT COMPROMISE YOUR FEMININITY FOR THE SAKE OF THE PULPIT

So, you were born female? Congratulations! God already knew your gender when the invitation to serve in the gospel ministry was issued. The call was not given just to be another one of the boys! The call was to preach, teach, pastor, or chaplain. The ministerial role takes priority over femaleness and maleness.

However, do not forsake your femininity. Do not surrender your femaleness, like Thecla, Joan of Arc, or Nzinga, to enhance a perception of power and authority. Do not leave your feminine self at the altar the day you enter seminary. Do not leave your feminine apparel on the altar the day of your ordination. Be feminine. Be you. Be real.

"If you want to look good, get your nails done, wear makeup and get your hair done, do it," said one single inner-city pastor. "And remember to have a life outside of the pulpit."

Clinical psychologist Dr. Henrietta Hestick indicates that in the pursuit of power, women in the ministry go through three developmental stages. The first stage is when women give up their gender for power. Women become neuter or neutral. Women in this stage tend to dress in a less-feminine manner and physically try to draw attention away from their femininity. They make statements like "It's not because I am a woman; forget that I am a woman, give me a job."[1]

Nzinga, the queen of Ngondo (Angola) dressed as a man, and her subjects addressed her as "King." Not until she was in her eighties, with her sister secured as her successor to the throne, did she felt secure enough to dress as a woman. She then dressed as an Amazon warrior in mock battle dress.[2]

The second stage is the opposite: asserting one's femininity. This stage emphasizes the feminine aspects of appearance and speech. Women in this stage are likely to say, "Look at who we are. We are women. We are different. This is a woman's issue."

The last stage is competence. This is reflected in attitude and statements such as "Give me the job, position, or church because I am competent, not because I am a woman and pretty."

Some feminine characteristics are assets in ministry. They include open communication, shared power, encouraging, supporting. It may do well to know the characteristics that belong to rigid transactional leadership styles, such as those that reflect paramilitary or athletic images. But you do not have to be a drill sergeant to be effective in ministry. It is a style that doesn't always work for those who do use it.

2. Thou Shall Not Be Intimidated by Those Who Question Your Call and Your Right to Be a Woman and a Minister

Whenever belief systems are challenged, no amount of evidence, biblical or otherwise, will ever be enough for some people. It will be what you do, not what you say that counts. It will be the demonstration of the power of God in your life, not constant proof texting, that will effectively challenge patriarchal paradigms. It will be your fruit, not your proof; it will be your gift, not your gab, that will make room for you. "Thou shall not be intimidated by male dominance and female jealousy. Thou shall hold your head up high and square your shoulders back," said a pastor.

Bishop Leontine Kelly states that we should not spend quality time on defending our call. Therefore be sure of your own theological position concerning women in the ministry. Be confident, not defensive, about your call to the gospel ministry. Remember that God, not humankind, issues the call to serve.

3. Thou Shall Be Wise in Establishing Personal Relationship within the Congregation

Maintain high moral standards and pastoral confidentiality. Be sure to walk in the best ministerial light, where all personal intentions are clear. The church is not a private dating agency or a harem for any man or woman. Do not place yourself in compromising positions. Be wary of those who hug too tightly, hold hands too long, or try to let the kiss on the cheek turn into something more. There are those who look for every opportunity to see you alone for "prayer and private consultation," indicated an associate minister. It is wise to have someone watch your back. It is wise to take officers with you on certain occasions and on visitations.

If you are single, "do not play where you pray." If you are married, remember your first ministry is in the home. "Be wise. There is a double standard. You cannot do what men do," said a pastor.

Be wise with female relationships in the church. "Conflict arises when women want to be my best friend. But I can't be every woman's best friend," said the pastor of a large Southern congregation. There are some women who would rather have you as a girlfriend than a pastor. They can handle you as girlfriend, not as pastor. These women and others will try things and do things to a female pastor that they would never do to a male minister.

"Understand your role as Corporate Mother," wrote a pastor of a 500-member church. "Pastor your church and keep house."

4. Thou Shall Not Be a Superwoman

Do not try to do it all yourself. There are some things that you cannot do and some things you will not want to do. Empower others to do these things.

A seminary professor said to me, "Do you want to live to see your grandchildren? You can't do it all, all the time."

Accentuate your gifts, wrote one pastor, and work on your limitations. Surround yourself with capable people who can help you in the areas where you are the weakest. And do not be afraid to use their expertise. Thou shall remember that Superman once died.

5. Thou Shall Be a Sister to Your Sister in the Ministry

Network, caucus, and pool your collective strength. There is still strength in unity. The hand is stronger than the finger. Two minds can be better than one, and much more can be done by some than one.

Look for opportunities to mentor other women. Share with women who have walked the rough road of ministry before you and are willing to share their wisdom and not just the gory details. Learn from the stories of other women. Learn to tell yours.

Try to build up and not tear down your sister in the ministry. There is enough to struggle with already without struggling with another sister. Do not allow men to put your sisters down publicly or privately.

"Thou shall not join male counterparts in putting women down. Thou shall be a part of the sisterhood. Just like the *Boyz in the Hood,* be 'Girls in the Hood.'" said Dr. Ruth Travis, pastor of Evergreen A.M.E. Church. "Thou shall not support ministries who deny women entrance to the ministry. Don't give them one dime! Thou shall support ministries which allow, accept, acknowledge, and support women in the ministry. Thou shall not let jealousy of another sister's gift make you miss a blessing. Thou shall celebrate a sister's gift."

6. Thou Shall Have African American Men as Brothers

There are plenty of brothers who support women in the ministry. There are plenty of men with whom you can develop a partnership and colleague-relationships. There are men who realize the strength of both genders standing together against common enemies. There are men who work in primary relationship with women in and for the unity of the African American community. We are still in this thing together!

"Thou shall know that every brother is not your friend or your enemy," said an associate minister. "Thou shall watch out for wolves in sheep's clothing."

"When I challenge White men on racism, they try to justify their reasons. The same is true with sexism. My response is that it is offensive to me as a Black woman. We shall not allow others to anticipate what our needs may be. In White denominational churches, they also define what your needs are. We cannot allow this to happen," said a former denominational staffer.

Men will collaborate with you. They will also compete for pulpits, assignments, perks, better positions, and power. "Temporal power is not given but taken. Just like freedom is not given but must be fought for and taken," said a woman who is a long-time denominational leader. She continued by observing that women pastors and female lay leaders who are perceived to have power are better liked than those with less power. Women pastors and female lay leaders who are perceived to have power are imitated more, have a higher self-concept, and are accepted more among colleagues than those with less, she said.

7. Be Assertive, Fair, and Firm

A "queen" may love to rule, and "Mama" may love to smother; but in the church, remember to be assertive, fair, and firm. Be humble before God and bold before God's adversaries. A minister must sometimes make hard decisions. They may be unpopular, but they must be made fairly and firmly. Being wishy-washy is just as bad as worrying. Worry is something you do that does not get you anywhere. Do not worry, pray. Be assertive, not a shrinking violet.

Develop your own leadership style. Read, observe, and take what works for you rather than imitating another's style. Learn to recognize which battles are yours to fight now and which ones are to be left alone or fought later. Ultimately, the battle belongs to God. "If God is in charge of the church, I go to sleep every night," wrote one pastor.

8. Thou Shall Not Oppress Others

The struggle for clergywomen is intense and often painful. Yet each minister must make a choice not to do to someone what has already been done to her. It would be so easy to find another group to plague. But vengeance belongs to God, and bitter soldiers do not receive sympathy.

A minister can act like Jezebel, a controlling manipulator who rose to the top over the bodies of her enemies, including her husband. Or she can act like Deborah, a decisive leader who demonstrated great people skills and role flexibility.

"Thou shall practice being nonbiased," said a suburban pastor. "Thou shall be an example of liberation toward others. Thou shall not enslave another with the same tired prejudices with which you were enslaved," said an urban associate minister.

9. Thou Shall Be a Role Model

"Thou shall ignore the microscope, but thou shall know that you are being watched night and day," states Dr. Travis.

"Thou shall show others the way. Teach what you know and reach back to take someone with, as you go," said an associate minister.

Remember, there are "Daughters of Thunder" coming behind you. Work courageously and bravely against limiting prophetic paradigms. In doing so, advantages will be gained and utilized. A foundation is laid for tomorrow by those serving today and demonstrating how it can be done.

10. Thou Shall Not Take Thyself Too Seriously

"Thou shall have a sense of humor," said one suburban pastor. "Thou shall frequently do a self-examination," said another.

Nothing lasts forever. The seasons do change. New ones will rush in with their own set of distinctions and characteristics. Learn to laugh a little to yourself and with others. Play a little to balance your workload. Walk, jump, run, swim, and eat and sleep right. Stop to smell the roses and to take hot bubble baths.

Maintenance is just as important as the mission. If a car is not properly maintained—with oil changes, tune-ups, gas in the tank, and air in the tires—it will not go far or run well. The same is true for humans. Take time for spiritual, mental, and emotional maintenance so you will be able to go far and run well.

If all of that is too hard to grasp when you are trying to balance responsibilities to God, husband, children, school, job, denominational officials, and significant others, just remember these four words of Rev. Cecelia Williams Bryant: "Relax, Retreat, Reflect, and Renew."

Chapter nine

EPILOGUE: WHERE DO WE GO FROM HERE?

THE AFRICAN AMERICAN church is just beginning to challenge sexism as a serious social concern. African American women are no long being treated as a momentary "fad" or "movement"; these women are pioneering equal access to ordained ministry and leadership positions traditionally held by male clergy.

Because the pool of available clergywomen is growing steadily, there is a need to give attention to their training and development. Women have not always had the privilege of training, preparation, and information.

Women ministers in general and African American clergywomen in particular may enjoy some measure of equal access to professional training and preparation. However, the challenge is to include in that preparation both gender-specific and gender-inclusive learning experiences. With these advantages, women will emerge as more competent, confident, and effective leaders.

The challenge is then threefold. We must first reclaim the legacy of female leadership from the margins of history. Retrieve the diaries, journals and stories from our eldest. Learn from the experiences of our ancestors to write new chapters of achievements today.

Second, we must strengthen the leadership skills of African American women in ministry. The challenge to the church in general is for a renewed commitment to biblical egalitarianism, which promotes the dignity and integrity of both men and women. Biblical egalitarianism elevates ideals drawn from Galatians 3:27–28 and Colossians 3:1–11. These two pericopes transform the shallow distinctions of race, class, cultural and social background, and gender into a new humanity.

This new humanity is biblical egalitarianism. It expresses itself in the form of a new person-sensitive universalism and unity. Gender differences do not mean that one is inferior or weaker and the other is superior or stronger. Each has inherent strengths, skills, and talents that must be respected. *Different*, then, means *unique*. Jesus Christ becomes the center of this new humanity. Egalitarianism emerges because "we are all one in Christ Jesus" (Gal. 3:28) and "Christ is all and in all" (Col. 3:11).

There is a need for this New Testament ideal regarding discrimination, class distinctions, freedom, racism, and sexism to be pushed to the front burner. The urgency is motivated by the male leadership in the church generally and the African American church specifically, who refuse to see sexism as a dehumanizing form just as evil as slavery and racism.

This egalitarianism can be manifested by a gender-inclusive biblical curriculum in college and seminary. A gender-inclusive curriculum is sensitive to and elevates the contributions of women in church history, the development of theological thought, biblical hermeneutics, leadership, and homiletics. This gender-inclusive curriculum should include published scholarly works by women in the academy. Students should also be exposed to visiting lecturers, preachers, and pastors who just happen to be female and doing great things.

There should be opportunities for both male and female students to experience female academic and clergy leadership. Students must be exposed to male and female role models who are open to dialogue and the exchange of ideas. The need for a gender-inclusive curriculum is not limited to the academy. Denominations and local churches should also conduct gender-inclusive training programs.

The challenge is to develop arenas that facilitate introducing female leadership into congregations, chaplaincies, ministries, and denominational positions that now have little or no exposure to female leadership. There is a need to examine the issues, such as sexism, that divide men and women in the ministry. The desired result would be the exploration and elevation of those things that unite us.

There is a need not only for learning experiences that are gender-inclusive, but for ones that are gender-specific as well. The results of the Learning Model, conducted in June 1992, and the Women in Ministry General Survey make a strong case for gender-specific courses and opportunities in the seminary experience and curriculum. There is also a challenge to develop gender-specific learning experiences in other church, denominational, and ministerial training programs.

Gender-specific experiences are those that foster confidence and assurance during the growth and development of female clergy. These experiences may include the development of caucuses and support groups; access to role models; and mentoring by female clergy, professors, and other professionals.

Gender-specific courses recommended are those mentioned in the survey. They include: Sexism and the African American Church; Managing Ministry and Family; The Impact of Physiological Changes and Women in Ministry; Preaching from a Female Perspective; Leadership Styles and Strategies for Women; Alternative Styles of Ministry; and Acclimating Congregations to Female Leadership.

Other suggested topics include: A Survey of the Role of African American Female Leadership in Church History; African American Women in Ministry; The Ordination of African American Women; Biblical Leadership Role Models for African American Women; and the Role of African American Women in Ministry in the Twenty-First Century.

My third recommendation is to include a learning experience for women in the ministry through retreats or workshops where role models can share advice and ideas. This recommendation is offered in light of budgetary limitations and the length of time it takes to review curriculum. This could be done in the academy or in denominational or local church settings.

The subject matter could vary depending on the interests of participants and/or the hosting body, but it would likely be drawn from those topics mentioned in gender-inclusive and gender-specific course offerings. Presenters would be those whose qualifications, egalitarianism, and availability recommend them. Many women have expressed a desire for an opportunity to dialogue with others on topics such as balancing ministry and family life; marriage and ministry; sexual harassment; handling conflicts; understanding men and power; and church polity and politics.

Another challenge is to explore gender-inclusive and gender-specific issues without eroding male-female relationships, during this transition, until the two separate entities lay down their swords to push the gospel plow together.

One of the greatest sources of frustration for women of African descent in America is having the door shut in our faces twice. The door of education, economic empowerment, career advancement, employment opportunity, and achievement is shut once for the color of our skin (racism) and again because of our gender (sexism).

Further, the frustration is the greatest when it is a member of our African American family who shuts the door the second time. It hurts most when the door is slammed by the ones with whom you have worked side by side for equality.

> The ones for whom you have championed the cause of liberation.
> The ones who have been bloodied and bowed with you to obtain justice at a great price.
> The ones who protested, picketed, signed petitions, and demonstrated with you.
> The family members who look like you and drink from the same cup of American apartheid with you.
> The ones who have tasted with you the bitter waters of segregation.
> The ones who faced the indignities of "colored-only" anything.
> The very ones who have known with you the anger and pain of community and corporate rejection.
> The ones who also felt the sting of a national policy of exclusion.
> The ones who know what it is like to be denied, pushed to the back of the bus of American life.
> The ones who know what it is like to be blamed for everything that is wrong with a community—crime, grime, welfare, and drugs.
> The ones who know what it is like to be the last hired and first fired.
> The ones who have been standing with you at the back of the line, generation after generation.
> The ones who know what it is like to be told "no," "never," "not yet," "wait and be patient."

The greatest frustration is seeing those whose hands you have held and helped to fight for a better community and church turn against you. They go through the door first and then close it in your face. It is not because you are incompetent, untrained, unskilled, unprepared, ignorant, or stupid; it is not because you haven't been called of God. It is because you are female. And then they tell you what they're doing is okay, because God says you're a second-class citizen.

There must be concern as long as the door is shut for any reason, racism or sexism. A community divided cannot stand.

Only the committed and continual strength of both genders, serving with each other and not pitted against each other, will propel us towards a biblical egalitarianism. The men will not make it without the women. The women will not go without the men. The struggle continues.

Notes

Introduction

1. Doug Murren, *Leadershift: How to Lead Your Church into the 21st Century by Managing Change* (Ventura, Calif.: Regal Books, 1994), 8–9, 125–32. For further discussion, see Stephen R. Covey, *The Seven Habits of Highly Effective People* (New York: Fireside/Simon & Schuster, 1990); see also Stephen R. Covey, A. Roger Merrill, and Rebecca R. Merrill, *First Things First* (New York: Simon & Schuster, 1994).

2. Delores C. Carpenter, "The Professionization of the Ministry of Women," *Journal of Religious Thought* 43, no. 1 (spring/summer 1986): 61.

3. Riane Eisler, *The Chalice and the Blade* (San Francisco: Harper, 1987), 28.

4. Patricia Aburdene and John Naisbitt, *Megatrends for Women* (New York: Villard Books, 1992), xxiv.

5. Ibid., xxii.

6. Ibid., 117.

7. Patricia Aburdene and John Naisbitt, *Megatrends for Women*, rev. ed. (New York: Fawcett Columbine, 1993), 128.

8. Ibid., 129.

9. Ibid.

10. C. Eric Lincoln and Lawrence H. Mamiya, *The Black Church in the African American Experience* (Durham, N.C.: Duke University Press, 1990), 289.

11. Carpenter, "The Professionalization of the Ministry of Women," 59.

12. Delores C. Carpenter, "Black Women in Religious Institutions," *Journal of Religious Thought* 46, no. 2 (winter/spring 1989–90): 25.

13. Lincoln and Mamiya, *The Black Church,* 301.

1. Historical Perspectives on Female Leadership in Greek, Roman, and Jewish Culture and Religion

1. Rosemary Ruether and Eleanor McLaughlin, *Women of Spirit: Female Leadership in the Jewish and Christian Traditions* (New York: Simon & Schuster, 1979), 16.

2. Carpenter, "The Professionalization of the Ministry of Women," 61.

3. Ibid.

4. Ruether and McLaughlin, *Women of Spirit*, 16–20.

5. Turid Karlsen Seim, *The Double Message: Patterns of Gender in Luke and Acts* (Nashville: Abingdon Press, 1994), 9–10.

6. Ibid.

7. Ivan Van Sertima, ed., *Black Women in Antiquity* (New Brunswick, N.J.: Transactional Books, 1988), 11.

8. Elizabeth Tetlow, *Women and Ministry in the New Testament* (New York: Paulist Press, 1980), 7.

9. Ibid.

10. Ibid., 8.

11. Ibid.

12. Wayne H. House, *The Role of Women in Ministry Today* (Nashville: Thomas Nelson, 1990), 55.

13. Tetlow, *Women and Ministry in the New Testament*, 11.

14. Ibid., 10.

15. Ibid., 11.

16. Ibid., 14.

17. Ibid., 16.

18. Wayne A. Meeks, *The First Urban Christians* (New Haven, Conn.: Yale University Press, 1993), 24.

19. Tetlow, *Women and Ministry in the New Testament*, 14–15.

20. Meeks, *The First Urban Christians*, 24–25.

21. Ibid., 25.

22. Tetlow, *Women and Ministry in the New Testament*, 20.

23. Ibid.

24. Ibid.

25. J. D. Douglas, ed., *The New Bible Dictionary* (Grand Rapids, Mich.: Eerdmans, 1977), 1336.

26. House, *The Role of Women in Ministry Today*, 66.

27. Ibid., 64.

28. Tetlow, *Women and Ministry in the New Testament*, 22.

29. Ibid., 23–24.

30. Tetlow, *Women and Ministry in the New Testament*, 22–23.

31. Ruether and McLaughlin, *Women of Spirit*, 17.

32. Tetlow, *Women and Ministry in the New Testament*, 21–22.

2. HISTORICAL PERSPECTIVES ON FEMALE LEADERSHIP IN AFRICAN CULTURE AND RELIGION

1. Van Sertima, *Black Women in Antiquity*, 11.

2. Oriaku Nwosu, *The African Woman: Nigerian Perspective* (Lagos: Bima Publications, Bima Africa Ltd., Integrated Press Ltd., 1993), 2, 14.

3. Ibid., 2, 15.

4. Oba T'Shaka, *Return to the African Mother Principle of Male and Female Equality,* vol. 1 (Oakland, Calif.: Pan Afrikan Publishers, 1995), 203.

5. Ibid., 204.

6. Rosalind Jeffries, "The Image of Woman in African Cave Art," in *Black Women in Antiquity*, ed. Van Sertima, 98.

7. John Henrik Clarke, "African Warrior Queens," in *Black Women in Antiquity*, ed. Van Sertima, 123.

8. Nwosu, *The African Woman,* 5–6.

9. Van Sertima, ed., *Black Women in Antiquity,* 5.

10. Ibid., 71.

11. Nwosu, *The African Woman,* 15.

12. T'Shaka, *Return to the African Mother Principle,* 205.

13. Ibid., 202.

14. Diedre Wimby, "The Female Horuses and Great Wives of Kemet," in *Black Women in Antiquity*, ed. Van Sertima, 41.

15. Nwosu, *The African Woman,* 15–16.

16. Sonia Sanchez, "Nefertiti: Queen to a Sacred Mission," in *Black Women in Antiquity*, ed. Van Sertima, 49.

17. Ibid., 54.

18. Van Sertima, *Black Women in Antiquity,* 7.

19. David Sweetman, *Women as Leaders in African History* (Portsmouth, N.H.: Heinemann Educational Books, 1994), 46.

20. Ibid., 10.

21. Ruether and McLaughlin, *Women of Spirit,* 22–23.

22. Van Sertima, *Black Women in Antiquity,* 6.

23. Cain H. Felder *Troubling Biblical Waters* (New York: Orbis Books, 1989), 34.

24. Larry Williams and Charles S. Finch, "The Great Queens of Ethiopia," in *Black Women in Antiquity*, ed. Van Sertima, 17–19.

25. Ibid., 11.

26. Nwosu, *The African Woman,* 3, 26.

27. Ibid., 3.

28. Ibid., 3, 26.

3. Historical Perspective on Female Leadership in the Church

1. Rosemary Radford Ruether and Rosemary Skinner Keller, eds., *In Our Own Voices: Four Centuries of American Women's Religious Writing* (New York: HarperCollins, 1995), 294–95.

2. Kay Mills, *From Pocahontas to Power Suits* (New York: Plume Books, 1995), 239.

3. Barbara Brown Zikmund, "Women and Ordination," in *In Our Own Voices*, ed. Ruether and Keller, 294.

4. Ibid., 69–71; Mills, *From Pocahontas to Power Suits*, 238.

5. Zikmund, "Women and Ordination," 71.

6. Jessie Carney Smith, *Black Firsts* (Detroit: Visible Ink Press, 1994), 312.

7. Mills, *From Pocahontas to Power Suits*, 239.

8. Nancy A. Hardesty, "Evangelical Women" in *In Our Own Voices*, ed. Ruether and Keller, 214–15.

9. Ruth A. Tucker and Walter Liefeld, *Daughters of the Church* (Grand Rapids, Mich.: Academic Books, Zondervan, 1987), 274.

10. Mills, *From Pocahontas to Power Suits*, 240.

11. Emilie M. Townes, "Black Women from Slavery to Womanist Liberation," in *In Our Own Voices*, ed. Ruether and Keller, 155.

12. Smith, *Black Firsts*, 328.

13. Townes, "Black Women," 158–59.

14. Ibid., 159.

15. Ibid.

16. Bert James Loewenberg and Ruth Bogin, eds. *Black Women in Nineteenth-Century American Life: Their Words, Their Thoughts, Their Feelings* (University Park: Pennsylvania State University Press, 1976), 134.

17. Ibid., 127.

18. Ibid.

19. Ibid., 135.

20. Ibid., 142.

21. Ibid., 143.

22. Zikmund, "Women and Ordination," 296–97.

23. Ibid., 297.

24. Smith, *Black Firsts*, 339.

25. Ibid.

26. Ibid., 305–6.

4. THEOLOGICAL PERSPECTIVE SUPPORTING AND REJECTING FEMALE LEADERSHIP

1. Jacquelyn Grant, *White Women's Christ and Black Women's Jesus* (Atlanta: Scholars Press, 1989), 10.

2. Ibid., 10. See also James Cone, *God of the Oppressed* (New York: Seabury Press, 1975), 39.

3. Grant, *White Women's Christ*, 9.

4. Ibid., 13.

5. Cain Hope Felder, *Stony the Road We Trod* (Maryknoll, N.Y.: Orbis Books, 1991), 6–7.

6. Grant, *White Women's Christ*, 209.

7. Renita J. Weems, "Reading Her Way through the Struggle: African American Women and the Bible," in *Stony the Road We Trod*, ed. Felder, 57–59. See also Grant, *White Women's Christ*, 211.

8. Elizabeth Schüssler Fiorenza, "Word, Spirit, and Power: Women in Early Christian Communities," in *In Our Own Voices*, ed. Ruether and Keller, 51.

9. Ibid., 55.

10. Ibid., 51–52.

11. Ibid., 53–54.

12. Rosemary Ruether, "Mother of the Church: Ascetic Women in the Late Patristic Age," in *In Our Own Voices*, ed. Ruether and Keller, 73.

13. Ibid., 74.

14. Fiorenza, "Word, Spirit, and Power," 57.

15. Ibid.

16. Henry Van Dyke, "Shall Women Be Licensed to Preach," *Homiletic Review* (1888): 24–31.

17. Grant, *White Women's Christ*, 25–26.

18. House, *The Role of Women in Ministry Today*, 11.

19. Ann Loades, *Feminist Theology: A Reader* (Louisville, Ky.: John Knox Press, 1990). 7.

20. Ibid., 1–3.

21. Ibid., 1. See also Gerda Lerner, *The Creation of Patriarchy* (New York: Oxford University Press, 1986), 236–37.

22. Loades, *Feminist Theology*, 2.

23. Cain Hope Felder, lecture delivered at Kelly Miller Smith Institute, Vanderbilt University, Nashville, Tenn., October 1992.

24. Denise Lardner Carmody, *Biblical Woman: Contemporary Reflections in Scriptual Texts* (New York: Crossroad, 1988), 127.

25. Lawrence O. Richards and Clyde Hoeldtke, *A Theology of Church Leadership* (Grand Rapids, Mich.: Zondervan, 1982), 21.

26. Ibid., 21.

27. Carmody, *Biblical Woman* , 133–36.

28. Felder, *Troubling Biblical Waters*, 52.

29. Patrick V. Rogers, *New Testament Message: A Biblical Theological Commentary*, ed. Wilfrid Harrington and Donald Senior (Wilmington, Del.: Michael Glazier, Inc., 1979): 61.

30. Fiorenza, "Word, Spirit, and Power," 57.

31. Grant, *White Women's Christ*, 104.

32. Lisa Sergio, *Jesus and Woman* (McLean, Va.: EPM Publications, 1975), 5.

33. Grant, *White Women's Christ*, 4–5.

34. Julia A. J. Foote, "A Brand Plucked from the Fire," in *Sisters of the Spirit,* ed. William Andrews (Bloomington: Indiana University Press, 1986), 209.

35. Weems, "Reading Her Way," 73.

36. Grant, *White Women's Christ*, 119.

37. Carmody, *Biblical Woman*, 146–47.

38. Grant, *White Women's Christ*, 21–22.

39. Patricia Hill Collins, *Black Feminist Thought,* vol. 2 (New York: Rutledge, 1991), 22.

40. Grant, *White Women's Christ,* 209.

41. Ibid., 210.

42. Gayaud Wilmore and James Cone, *Black Theology: A Documentary History, 1966–1979* (New York: Orbis, 1979), 365.

43. Ibid.

44. Grant, *White Women's Christ,* 210.

45. Ibid., 219.

5. BIBLICAL IMAGES OF FEMALE LEADERSHIP

1. Frank Chikane, *No Life of My Own* (New York: Orbis Books, 1988), 13.

2. Felder, *Troubling Biblical Waters,* 48.

3. Weems, "Reading Her Way," 59.

4. Ibid., 57.

5. Alice J. Laffey, *An Introduction to the Old Testament* (Philadelphia: Fortress Press, 1988), 2–3.

6. Ibid., 3.

7. Ibid.

8. Felder, *Stony the Road We Trod,* 7.

9. C. W. Hall, *Samuel Logan Brengle* (New York: Salvation Army, 1933), 3. See also J. Oswald Sanders, *Spiritual Leadership* (Chicago: Moody Press, 1967), 20.

10. Nancy Hastings, "Let Pharaoh Go," in *And Blessed Is She,* ed. David A. Farmer and Edwina Hunter (San Francisco: Harper & Row, 1994).

11. Schüssler Fiorenza, "Word, Spirit, and Power," 33.

12. Ibid., 34.

13. Ibid., 36–37.

14. Ibid., 34–36.

15. Ibid., 36.

16. Ibid., 33–37.

6. LEADERSHIP STYLES AND BIBLICAL ROLE MODELS

1. Norman Shawchuck and Roger Heuser, *Leading the Congregation: Caring for Yourself While Serving Others* (Nashville, Tenn.: Abingdon Press, 1993) 261.

2. Floyd Massey Jr. and Samuel B. McKinney, *Church Administration in the Black Perspective* (Valley Forge, Pa.: Judson Press, 1976), 37.

3. Ibid., 12.

4. Cornel West, *Prophetic Fragments* (Grand Rapids, Mich.: Eerdmans, 1988), 88.

5. Ibid.

6. James H. Harris, *Black Ministers and Laity in the Urban Church* (Lanham, Md.: University Press of America, 1987), 7.

7. James D. Lawson, *Leadership Is Everybody's Business* (n.p.: Impact Publishers, 1976), 176.

8. Robert D. Dale, *Pastoral Leadership* (Nashville, Tenn.: Abingdon Press, 1986), 13.

9. Massey and McKinney, *Church Administration*, 25–26.

10. Thomas C. Campbell and Gary B. Reierson, *The Gift of Administration* (Philadelphia: Westminster Press, 1981), 18–19.

11. Dale, *Pastoral Leadership*, 14.

12. Lawson, *Leadership Is Everybody's Business*, 178.

13. Dale, *Pastoral Leadership*, 39.

14. Ibid., 226.

15. Beth Milwid, *Working with Men* (New York: Berkeley Books, 1993), 40.

16. Ibid., 43.

17. Ibid., 22.

18. Patricia Aburdene and John Naisbitt, *Megatrends for Women* (New York: Fawcett Columbine, 1993), 99–101; Judy B. Rosener, in *Harvard Business Review* (November/December 1990): 119.

19. Dale, *Pastoral Leadership*, 40–41.

20. Ibid., 42.

21. Ibid., 44.

22. Ibid.

23. Ibid., 45.

24. Ibid., 42.

25. Ibid., 43.

26. *The Authorized Daily Prayer Book* (London: Valentine and Co., 1947), 21.

27. Laffey, *Introduction to the Old Testament*, 2.

28. Gein Karssen, *Her Name Is Woman* (Colorado Springs, Colo.: Nav Press, 1975), 115.

29. Williams and Finch, "The Great Queens of Ethiopia," 16.

30. Ibid., 17.

31. Ibid.

7. A Profile of African American Women in the Ministry and Womanist Leader-Style Response

1. Milwid, *Working with Men*, 48.

2. Ibid., 167.

3. Ibid., 168–69.

4. Lyle Schaller, ed., *Women as Pastors* (Nashville: Abingdon, 1982), 110.

8. Ten Commandments for African American Women in the Ministry

1. Henrietta Hestick, "Women Surviving in Ministry" seminar, Payne Memorial A.M.E. Church, Baltimore, Md., June 1992.

2. Sweetman, *Women as Leaders in African History*, 46–47.

BIBLIOGRAPHY

Aburdene, Patricia, and John Naisbitt. *Megatrends for Women*. Rev. ed. New York: Fawcett Columbine, 1993.

———. *Megatrends for Women*. New York: Vallard Books, 1992.

Adams, Arthur Merrihew. *Effective Leadership for Today's Church*. Philadelphia: Westminster Press, 1978.

Anderson, James D., and Ezra E. Jones. *The Management of Ministry*. San Francisco: Harper & Row, 1978.

Andrews, William L. *Sisters of the Spirit: Three Black Women's Autobiographies of the Nineteenth Century*. Bloomington: Indiana University Press, 1986.

The Authorized Daily Prayer Book. London: Valentine & Co., 1947.

Bennett, G. Willis. *Effective Urban Church Ministry*. Nashville, Tenn.: Broadman Press, 1983.

Bennis, Warren. *The Unconscious Conspiracy: Why Leaders Can't Lead*. New York: AMACOM, 1976.

Burns, James MacGregor. *Leadership*. New York: Harper & Row, 1978.

Callahan, Kennon L. *Effective Church Leadership*. San Francisco: HarperCollins, 1990.

———. *Twelve Keys to an Effective Church*. New York: Harper & Row, 1983.

Campbell, Thomas C., and Gary B. Reierson. *The Gift of Administration*. Philadelphia: Westminster Press, 1981.

Cannon, Katie. *Black Womanist Ethics*. Atlanta: Scholars Press, 1985.

Carmody, Denise Lardner. *Biblical Woman: Contemporary Reflections in Scriptual Texts*. New York: Crossroad, 1988.

Carpenter, Delores C. "Black Women in Religious Institutions." *Journal of Religious Thought* 46, no. 2 (winter/spring 1989–90): 7–27.

———. "The Professionlization of the Ministry of Women." *Journal of Religious Thought* 43, no. 1 (spring/summer 1986): 59–75.

Chikane, Frank. *No Life of My Own*. Maryknoll, N.Y.: Orbis Books, 1988.

Clarke, John Henrik. "African Warrior Queens." In *Black Women in Antiquity*, edited by Ivan Van Sertima. New Brunswick, N.J.: Transactional Books, 1987.

Collins, Patricia Hill. *Black Feminist Thought.* New York: Routledge, 1990.

Cornwall, Judson. *Let Us Worship.* South Plainfield, N.J.: Bridge Publishing, 1983.

Covey, Stephen R. *The Seven Habits of Highly Effective People.* New York: Fireside Books/Simon & Schuster, 1989.

Covey, Stephen R., A. Roger Merrill, and Rebecca R. Merrill. *First Things First.* New York: Simon & Schuster, 1994.

Cueni, R. Robert, and Herb Miller. *The Vital Church Leader.* Nashville, Tenn.: Abingdon Press, 1991.

Dale, Robert D. *Ministers as Leaders.* Nashville, Tenn.: Broadman Press, 1994.

————. *Pastoral Leadership.* Nashville, Tenn.: Abingdon Press, 1986.

DePree, Max. *Leadership Is an Art.* New York: Dell Publishing, 1989.

Douglas, J. D. *The New Bible Dictionary.* Grand Rapids, Mich.: Eerdmans, 1973.

Eisler, Riane. *The Chalice and the Blade.* San Francisco: Harper, 1987.

Engstrom, Ted W., and Edward R. Dayton. *The Art of Management for Christian Leaders.* Grand Rapids, Mich.: Zondervan, 1989.

Farmer, David A., and Edwina Hunter, eds. *And Blessed Is She.* San Francisco: Harper & Row, 1994.

Felder, Cain Hope. *Stony the Road We Trod.* Maryknoll, N.Y.: Orbis Books, 1991.

————, ed. *Troubling Biblical Waters.* Maryknoll, N.Y.: Orbis Books, 1989.

Fiedler, Fred E., and Martin M. Chemers. *Improving Leadership Effectiveness: The Leadermatch Concept.* New York: John Wiley & Sons, 1976.

Fiorenza, Elizabeth. "Word, Spirit and Power: Women in Early Christian Communities." In *In Our Own Voices: Four Centuries of American Women's Religious Writing,* edited by Rosemary Radford Ruether and Rosemary Skinner Keller. San Francisco: HarperCollins, 1995.

Foote, Julia A. J. "A Brand Plucked from the Fire." In *Sisters of the Spirit,* edited by William Andrews. Bloomington: Indiana University Press, 1986.

Ford, Leighton. *Transforming Leadership.* Downer's Grove, Ill.: InterVarsity, 1992.

Furnish, Victor. *The Moral Teaching of Paul.* Nashville: Abingdon, 1979.

Goodwin, Bennie. *The Effective Leader.* Downer's Grove, Ill.: InterVarsity Press, 1981.

Grant, Jacquelyn. *White Women's Christ and Black Women's Jesus.* Atlanta: Scholars Press, 1989.

Hall, C. W. *Samuel Logan Brengle.* New York: Salvation Army, 1933.

Hardesty, Nancy A. "Evangelical Women." In *In Our Own Voices: Four Centuries of American Women's Religious Writing,* edited by Rosemary Radford Ruether and Rosemary Skinner Keller. San Francisco: HarperCollins, 1995.

Harris, James H. *Black Ministers and Laity in the Urban Church*. Lanham, Md.: University Press of America, 1987.

Hastings, Nancy. "Let Pharoah Go." In *And Blessed Is She*, edited by David A. Farmer and Edwina Hunter. San Francisco: Harper & Row, 1994.

Hestick, Henrietta. "Women in Ministry" seminar speech. Payne Memorial A.M.E. Church, Baltimore, Md., 1992.

Hodgson, Peter C., and Robert H. King, eds., *Christian Theology*. Philadelphia: Fortress Press, 1982.

House, Wayne H. *The Role of Women in Ministry Today*. Nashville, Tenn.: Thomas Nelson Publishers, 1990.

Hull, Gloria T., Patricia S. Bell, and Barbara Smith. *But Some of Us Are Brave: Black Women's Studies*. New York: Feminist Press, 1982.

Hunsaker, Phillip L. Allessandra. *The Art of Managing People*. Englewood Cliffs, N.J.: Prentice-Hall, 1980.

Jeffries, Rosalind. "The Image of Woman in African Cave Art." In *Black Women in Antiquity*, edited by Ivan Van Sertima. New Brunswick, N.J.: Transactional Books, 1987.

Karssen, Gien. *Her Name Is Woman*. Colorado Springs, Colo.: Nav Press, 1975.

Keating, Charles J., *The Leadership Book*. New York: Paulist Press, 1978.

Kouzes, James M., and Barry Z. Posner. *The Leadership Challenge*. San Francisco: Jossey-Bass, 1995.

Ladner, Joyce. *Tomorrow's Tomorrow: The Black Woman*. Garden City, N.Y.: Doubleday, 1971.

Laffey, Alice. *An Introduction to the Old Testament*. Philadelphia: Fortress Press, 1988.

Lawson, John D., *Leadership Is Everybody's Business*. N.p.: Impact Publishers, 1976.

Lerner, Gerda. *The Creation of Patriarchy*. New York: Oxford University Press, 1986.

Lincoln, C. Eric, and Lawrence H. Mamiya. *The Black Church in the African American Experience*. Durham, N.C.: Duke University Press, 1990.

Loades, Ann, ed. *Feminist Theology: A Reader*. Louisville, Ky.: SPCK, 1990.

Lowenberg, Bert James, and Ruth Bogin. *Black Women in Nineteenth Century American Life: Their Words, Their Thoughts, Their Feelings*. University Park: Pennsylvania State University Press, 1976.

Lutz, Robert H., and Bruce T. Taylor. *Surviving in Ministry*. New York: Paulist Press, 1990.

Massey, Floyd, Jr., and Samuel B. McKinney. *Church Administration in the Black Perspective*. Valley Forge, Pa.: Judson Press, 1976.

Matthews, Mark D. "Our Women and What They Think." *The Black Scholar* 8/9 (May/June 1979): 2–13.

Meeks, Wayne A. *The First Urban Christians*. New Haven, Conn.: Yale University Press, 1983.

Mills, Kay. *From Pocahontas to Power Suits*. New York: Plume Book, 1995.

Milwid, Beth. *Working with Men*. New York: Berkley Books, 1990.

Mosley, Ernest E. *Leadership Profiles from Bible Personalities*. Nashville, Tenn.: Broadman Press, 1979

Murren, Doug. *Leadshift: How to Lead Your Church into the 21st Century by Managing Change*. Ventura, Calif.: Regal Books, 1994.

Noble, Jeanne. *Beautiful, Also, Are the Souls of My Black Sisters*. Englewood Cliffs, N.J.: Prentice-Hall, 1981.

Nwosu, Oriaku. *The African Woman: Nigerian Perspective*. Lagos: Bima Publications, Bima Africa Ltd., 1993.

Peters, Thomas J., and Robert H. Waterman Jr. *In Search of Excellence: Lessons from America's Best-Run Companies.* New York: Harper & Row, 1992.

Peterson, Eugene H. *Five Smooth Stones for Pastoral Work*. Atlanta: John Knox Press, 1975.

Richards, Lawrence O., and Cylde Hoeldtke. *A Theology of Church Leadership*. Grand Rapids, Mich.: Zondervan, 1980.

Rogers, Patrick V. *New Testament Message: A Biblical Theological Commentary*. N.p.: Michael Glazier, 1980.

Ruether, Rosemary. "Mother of the Church: Ascetic Women in the Late Patristic Age." In *In Our Own Voices: Four Centuries of American Women's Religious Writing,* edited by Rosemary Radford Ruether and Rosemary Skinner Keller. San Francisco: HarperCollins, 1995.

Ruether, Rosemary Radford, and Rosemary Skinner Keller, eds. *In Our Own Voices: Four Centuries of American Women's Religious Writing.* San Francisco: HarperCollins, 1995.

Ruether, Rosemary, and Eleanor McLaughlin. *Women of Spirit: Female Leadership in the Jewish and Christian Traditions.* New York: Simon & Schuster, 1979.

Sanchez, Sonia. "Nefertiti: Queen to a Sacred Mission." In *Black Women in Antiquity*, edited by Ivan Van Sertima. New Brunswick, N.J.: Transactional Books, 1987.

Sanders, J. Oswald. *Spiritual Leadership*. Chicago: Moody Press, 1967.

Schaller, Lyle. *Women as Pastors*. Nashville, Tenn.: Abingdon, 1982.

Seim, Turid Karlsen. *The Double Message: Patterns of Gender in Luke and Acts.* Nashville, Tenn.: Abingdon, 1994.

Sergio, Lisa. *Jesus and Woman*. McLean, Va.: EPM Publications, 1975.

Shawchuck, Norman, and Roger Heuser. *Leading the Congregation.* Nashville, Tenn.: Abingdon, 1993.

Smith, Betsy Covington. *Breakthrough Women in Religion*. New York: Walker & Company, 1978.

Smith, Bob. *When All Else Fails . . . Read the Directions: Considering God's Plan for a Living Church*. Waco, Tex.: Word Books Publishers, 1974.

Smith, Jessie Carney. *Black Firsts*. Detroit: Visible Ink Press, 1994.

Stendahl, Krister. *The Bible and the Role of Women: Facet Books Biblical Series No. 15*. Philadelphia: Fortress Press, 1966.

Sweetman, David. *Women as Leaders in African History*. Portsmouth, N.H.: Heineman Educational Books, 1984.

Tanner, Benjamin T. "The Organization of Women A.M.E. Church." *The A.M.E. Review* (April 1886): 452–78.

Tetlow, Elizabeth M. *Women and Ministry in the New Testament*. New York: Paulist Press, 1980.

Thomas, Latta. *Biblical Faith and the Black American*. Valley Forge, Pa.: Judson Press, 1976.

Townes, Emilie M. "Black Women from Slavery to Womanist Liberation." In *In Our Own Voices: Four Centuries of American Women's Religious Writing*, edited by Rosemary Radford Ruether and Rosemary Skinner Keller. San Francisco: HarperCollins, 1995.

T'Shaka, Oba. *Return to the African Mother Principle of Male and Female Equality*. Oakland, Calif.: Pan Afrikan Pubishers, 1995.

Tucker, Ruth A., and Walter Liefeld. *Daughters of the Church*. Grand Rapids, Mich.: Zondervan, 1987.

Van Dyke, Henry. "Shall Women Be Licensed to Preach," *Homiletic Review* (1888): 24–31.

Van Sertima, Ivan, ed. *Black Women in Antiquity*. New Brunswick, N.J.: Transactional Books, 1987.

Verdesi, Elizabeth. *In but Still Out*. Philadelphia: Westminster Press, 1976.

Wahlbert, Rachel Conrad. *Jesus According to a Woman*. New York: Paulist Press, 1975.

Walrath, Douglas Alan. *Leading the Church through Changes*. Nashville, Tenn.: Abingdon Press, 1979.

Watterson, Andrew. *Pastoral Leadrship*. Nashville, Tenn.: Abingdon Press, 1949.

Weems, Renita J. "Reading Her Way through the Struggle: African American Women and the Bible." In *Stony the Road We Trod*, edited by Cain Hope Felder. Maryknoll, N.Y.: Orbis Books, 1991.

West, Cornel. *Prophetic Fragments*. Grand Rapids, Mich.: Eerdmans, 1988.

White, Joseph L., and Thomas A. Parham. *The Psychology of Blacks: An African American Perspective*. Englewood Cliffs, N.J.: Prentice-Hall, 1990.

White, Robert. *Managing Today's Church*. Valley Forge, Pa.: Judson Press, 1982.

Wilmore, Gayraud S., and James H. Cone. *Black Theology: A Documentary History, 1966–1979.* Maryknoll, N.Y.: Orbis Books, 1979.

Wimby, Diedre. "The Female Horuses and Great Wives of Kemet." In *Black Women in Antiquity*, edited by Ivan Van Sertima. New Brunswick, N.J.: Transactional Books, 1987.

Zikmund, Barbara Brown. "Women and Ordination." In *In Our Own Voices: Four Centuries of American Women's Religious Writing*, edited by Rosemary Radford Ruether and Rosemary Skinner Keller. San Francisco: HarperCollins, 1995.